RAND

European Defense and the Future of Transatlantic Cooperation

Scott A. Harris, James B. Steinberg

Prepared for the
Under Secretary of Defense for Policy

**National Defense
Research Institute**

PREFACE

This report was prepared as part of the project "Emerging Issues in the Debate over a European Security Identity and Implications for U.S. Policy," sponsored by the Under Secretary of Defense for Policy. The project is being conducted in the International Security and Defense Strategy Program within RAND's National Defense Research Institute, a federally funded research and development center sponsored by the Office of the Secretary of Defense and the Joint Staff.

In addition to the sources cited in this report, the authors conducted extensive interviews with government officials and nongovernmental experts in Europe and the United States during 1992 and early 1993. The cutoff point for information on which this report is based is June 1993.

CONTENTS

SUMMARY

With the fall of the Berlin Wall and the unification of Germany, the demise of the Warsaw Treaty Organization, and, ultimately, the collapse of the Soviet Union, the United States and its allies in the North Atlantic Treaty Organization (NATO) are facing a new security environment, requiring new structures and institutions, and a new definition of roles and responsibilities for mutual security. NATO has taken a number of steps in this direction, including reorganizing its military command structure, reducing the size of its standing military forces, and changing the way NATO forces are organized and deployed, with new emphasis on multinational formations and mobility. The United States and other NATO allies are reducing their forces.

Simultaneous with the rapidly changing security environment, the twelve members of the European Community (EC) moved to closer integration with the Maastricht Treaty on European Union in December 1991, which, *inter alia*, commits the European Community to develop a common foreign and security policy (CFSP), which will lead to a common defense policy and could result in a common European defense.

The need to restructure European security organizations and EC moves to strengthen economic and political unity have led to efforts to create a European "identity" in security and defense. The United States has welcomed efforts to create a stronger European pillar, both as a means of reducing the U.S. burden of European defense and as a means of creating a more capable partner for the United States in possible military operations outside the NATO area (e.g., a future Desert Storm). European views of the EDI have differed, with France tending to emphasize the EDI as an element of European Union while the United Kingdom places greater emphasis on the EDI as a complement to NATO. Germany favors both conceptions, at times emphasizing one more than the other, and this dual approach was endorsed by the Western European Union in December 1991.

1992: ORGANIZING THE EUROPEAN DEFENSE IDENTITY

Following the NATO and EC summits in 1991, European governments struggled over competing approaches to constructing the EDI. France and Germany proposed creating a European Corps organized around a nucleus of French and German forces. Kohl and Mitterrand announced their detailed plan for establishing this Corps in May 1992, despite criticism from London and Washington. The Corps will assume its operational capabilities over the next three years. Belgium agreed to participate in the spring of 1993, and Spanish participation is likely by 1994. Although the proposal for the Corps initially concerned the United States and "Atlanticist" European states that it could undermine NATO, a December 1992 agreement between France, Germany, and NATO has largely dissipated those concerns and opened the prospect that, for the first time since France left the integrated command in 1966, French troops will serve under NATO operational command.

The Western European Union meeting in June 1992 announced a plan to provide an operational role for the EDI along a model proposed earlier by the British and the Italians. This concept foresees a menu of member states' forces available to the WEU for use in contingencies, but no standing forces under WEU command in peacetime. These forces could be used for missions ranging from peacekeeping to crisis management or "peacemaking." The WEU agreed to establish a Planning Cell at Brussels and moved its headquarters from London to Brussels. The WEU demonstrated its willingness to undertake autonomous operations by agreeing to dispatch a small force in the Adriatic to monitor the embargo on Serbia, a deployment matched by NATO. The WEU has also taken steps to expand its relationship with the countries of Eastern Europe.

THE EDI AND THE UNITED STATES

The United States has broadly endorsed the development of the EDI as a strengthened pillar for the Atlantic Alliance, supporting the British approach to base the EDI on a strengthened operational role for the WEU. This conception contributes to achieving the key U.S. goals of retaining NATO's primacy as the forum for security discussions among the Allies and as the exclusive means for organizing the defense of NATO territory, while strengthening the ability of the European Allies to act outside the NATO area, either as a partner of the United States or independently if the United States chooses not to act.

U.S. policy toward the EDI should focus on achieving five enduring U.S. interests:

- Prevent the emergence of a direct threat to the United States;

- Preserve the security and stability of the Euro-Atlantic area;

- Maintain and strengthen the U.S.-European partnership in responding to security problems outside Europe;

- Retain U.S. influence to shape policies in a way that will promote U.S. global political and economic interests; and

- Reduce the U.S. burden associated with European defense.

Neither the United States nor the European Community can achieve these objectives acting alone. Therefore, the United States needs a two-pronged strategy: foster NATO's evolution to maintain its relevance and effectiveness while seeking to shape the emerging EDI in ways compatible with U.S. interests and objectives. There are five key elements to this strategy:

(1) Continue to support the EDI;

(2) Continue to work to shape the Eurocorps' development in ways that are compatible with NATO and with U.S. security interests;

(3) Adapt NATO to embrace an effective EDI and build links between the EDI and NATO;

(4) Begin to identify the respective roles of NATO and the EDI, but avoid establishing formal or binding criteria; and

(5) Try to preserve the congruence in membership between NATO and the EDI, but accept that the EDI can become the defense arm of the EC.

An EDI can reduce the U.S. security burden and firm up U.S. forces for other contingencies, and provide a militarily strong partner for operations beyond NATO territory.

Opposing the Franco-German Corps will harm relations with key allies without commensurate benefits. The near-term risk that the Corps will undermine NATO is small. Rather than trying to block it, the United States should support efforts to bind the Corps to the WEU and to NATO.

Domestic political and budgetary pressures as well as external events will force NATO to evolve, but maintaining a reformed NATO serves important U.S. interests. The political functions of the Alliance, as the essential forum for consultation on matters of common security interests, are important to the United States. The United States can accept a more equal role in the Alliance, provided the collective responsibilities are shared more equally. The United States must seek to avoid the alternative: unilateral European actions affecting U.S. interests on which the United States was not consulted.

NATO must continue to adapt organizationally as well, to ensure that NATO can operate effectively in both its traditional area and potential out-of-area missions. An EDI organized around the WEU with an effective operational role complements this objective for NATO. Close links between the EDI/WEU and NATO are therefore essential, to avoid duplication, to develop the capacity for Europeans to act with minimal or no U.S. involvement in some contingencies, and to ensure that if major contingencies arise the Alliance retains the necessary military capability. To facilitate independent European action where appropriate, the EDI should be built around dual-hatted European forces, answerable to the WEU and to NATO; the European Deputy SACEUR and Chief of Staff should be dual-hatted as well, as WEU Commander and Chief of Staff. Close liaison between the SHAPE staff and the WEU's Planning Cell, as well as close consultations in the Alliance and through the secretariats, can lead to a workable division of roles and responsibilities. For future missions, such as peacekeeping or peacemaking, these structural adaptations are essential.

An EDI that developed into the defense arm of the European Community would not necessarily harm U.S. interests, so long as the EC does not neglect the security needs of Central and Eastern European countries. As the emerging democracies in Central and Eastern Europe develop links with the EDI, the United States should support extending NATO ties as well, including NATO membership to preserve the congruence of the EC and NATO security guarantees.

ACKNOWLEDGMENTS

The authors would like to thank Mr. Martin McCusker, Director of the North Atlantic Assembly's Defence and Security Subcommittee, and RAND colleagues Richard Kugler, Denise Quigley, and Doris Siegel for their comments and assistance in preparing this study. We are also grateful to officials from France, Germany, the United Kingdom, NATO, and the European Community who gave generously of their time and expertise.

Chapter One

A EUROPEAN DEFENSE IDENTITY AND TRANSATLANTIC SECURITY COOPERATION

The European security environment has changed radically in the months since the fall of the Berlin Wall, the collapse of the Warsaw Treaty Organization as a military alliance, and the demise of the Soviet Union. The absence, after more than forty years, of a militarily strong, superpower adversary, capable of conducting large-scale conventional and nuclear warfare, has forced the United States and its European allies to reevaluate the Cold War assumptions and structures of Western security policy. In the United States, the newly elected Clinton Administration is continuing the process of redefining U.S. interests and the future U.S. role in European security. The need for links between the United States and Europe, a cornerstone of U.S. policy for forty years, now must be redefined and articulated in the new context, and longstanding relationships renewed or revised. The member states of the North Atlantic Treaty Organization (NATO), the pre-eminent Western Cold War security alliance, are seeking to define the organization's roles and purposes in the post-Cold War world. Nations are also examining the possible roles of other organizations such as the Western European Union (WEU) and the Conference on Security and Cooperation in Europe (CSCE) in contributing to European security. To the east, states formerly locked into the orthodoxy of the Warsaw Pact now seek fresh approaches for assuring their security. New organizations such as the North Atlantic Cooperation Council (NACC) have emerged to address problems created by the collapse of the old order.

The end of the Cold War security order has contributed to, and also complicated, the process of political and economic integration in Europe. German leaders have intensified their efforts to embed

1

Germany in a web of European institutions to reassure allies and former adversaries that unified Germany will pose no new threat to European security. This strategy has led Germany to reaffirm its commitment to NATO and enthusiastically pursue other security ties, notably with France. In addition to security linkages, Germany continued to work to deepen the European Community in a process that culminated in the agreement reached at Maastricht, Netherlands in December 1991. The Maastricht Treaty on European Union commits the members of the European Community not only to economic and monetary union by the end of the century, but also to begin to forge a common foreign and security policy (CFSP), the first step on what could prove to be a path toward a common European defense.

Whether to create a distinctive European security and defense identity is thus part of the wider effort to redefine and redirect existing security institutions. In its most general terms this effort is supported by the United States as an appropriate response to the collapse of the bipolar Cold War world and as an important adjunct to the growing economic and political links among the European Community member states.

During 1992 it became clear that ratifying the Maastricht Treaty, not to mention realizing its ambitious objectives, including those in the security and defense spheres, was not, as most originally thought, a mere formality. Following Danish voters' rejection of the treaty, it narrowly survived a referendum in France and faced serious obstacles in Britain. Moreover, governments in the five largest EC states faced political crises throughout 1992 and early 1993, including the collapse of the Italian political structure and the resounding electoral defeat of the governing Socialist Party in France. These political difficulties also had the effect of slowing down the Maastricht process.

While European governments now generally agree that some form of an enhanced European security and defense identity is desirable, they continue to debate, sometimes contentiously, its precise role and institutional structures. This debate is in part about the structure of political influence in post–Cold War Europe. France, for example, seeks to give the EDI a strong "European" flavor, premised at least in part on the belief that Europe cannot and should not depend on substantial American involvement in European security in the future. Many, both in and outside Germany, see the debate as one about how to channel and direct the power of unified Germany. Most British officials, and like-minded leaders in the Netherlands, Denmark, and Portugal, see the debate over the EDI as part of the larger issue of whether a common foreign and security policy or a common defense policy for Europe is desirable, or even possible, independent of transatlantic structures. The United Kingdom seeks to assure that as, and if, the EDI develops, Britain is not marginalized in Europe and that the Atlantic Alliance remains intact. For Britain, this means placing greater emphasis on the European contribution to Euro-Atlantic security, the European "pillar" of the Atlantic Alliance, rather than on the development of a separate "European" identity.

The effort to construct a European security and defense identity faces practical as well as theoretical obstacles. While European policymakers debate the competing conceptions of EDI, the unfolding crisis on their doorstep in former Yugoslavia threatens to make a mockery of their discussions. At the very moment that the Twelve were agreeing in principle to a common foreign and security policy at Maastricht in late 1991, their divided response to the Yugoslavia crisis demonstrated how far they had to go to make common policy a working reality. Only the threat that Germany would act unilaterally (just days after the Maastricht summit) galvanized the rest of the EC to recognize the breakup of Yugoslavia and the independence of Slovenia and Croatia. While the nine members of the WEU agreed to create a new planning cell for common actions, they have reached little agreement on using military force in Bosnia, even to protect humanitarian convoys.

The debate over the European defense identity raises fundamental issues about the future of the U.S.-European relationship. In the security sphere, this relationship has been centered on the North Atlantic Treaty Organization (NATO) for more than forty years. As the Allies celebrate their "victory" in the Cold War, they also face inevitable questions concerning the Alliance's continued relevance in the face of markedly diminished threats. Legislatures and publics, eager to taste tangible benefits from reduced tensions and to ease the burden of military spending, seek reduced military forces and defense budgets. While the NATO allies have shown no desire to disband or terminate the Alliance, they have taken steps to reduce the size of the standing forces and to reorganize the Alliance command structure. Where NATO will fit in the new architecture of European security is an important element in the debate over the European defense identity, and an important determinant of the future U.S. role.

The United States is affected by the debate over the European defense identity, not only because of its role in and leadership of NATO, but also because of the larger security interests it shares with its European allies. The United States has an interest in pursuing common security objectives with Europeans, and not only for the defense of NATO territory (as, for example, in the Gulf War). How the Europeans choose to define their security and defense identity is therefore a matter of considerable policy significance for the United States. Although the United States has supported a stronger, more coherent European defense identity since the early years of the Cold War, the form and shape of an EDI could have especially important consequences in the post–Cold War era, either as the basis for a new security relationship or as an impetus to a widening Atlantic gulf. How the United States responds to or participates in debate over EDI could have significant implications for long-term U.S. interests and influence, globally as well as in Europe.

Chapter Two of this report analyzes the evolution of the debate over the European defense identity, both within Europe and in the transatlantic context of NATO, leading to the Rome NATO and Maastricht EC summits in the fall of 1991. Chapter Three discusses in detail the issues raised post-Maastricht, with particular emphasis on the Western European Union and the Franco-German ("European") Corps as these issues played out in 1992 and early 1993. Finally, Chapter Four identifies the implications of various alternative formulations of the European defense identity for U.S. long-term interests and objectives in Europe and outlines a strategy for achieving those objectives.

Chapter Two

EVOLUTION OF THE CONCEPT OF A EUROPEAN DEFENSE IDENTITY

Over the past three years, two major international developments—the collapse of the Soviet internal and external empires, and the movement toward deeper integration in the European Community—have driven the evolution of Western security strategy and structures and motivated the debate over the need for, and role of, a European defense identity. This evolution is reflected in key policy decisions adopted by the principal West European political institutions—NATO, the EC, and the WEU.

DAWN OF THE POST–COLD WAR ERA

When the North Atlantic Council met in London in July 1990, NATO leaders understood the need to change the Alliance's political concept and military strategy. EDI was a element of the reformation, even in the earliest days of the post–Cold War debates, as the "London Declaration on a Transformed North Atlantic Alliance," issued at the end of the summit by NATO's heads of state and government, shows. Noting that a unified Germany in the "heart of Europe" meant the end of Europe's division, the Allies declared that

> the move within the European Community towards political union, including the development of a European identity in the domain of security, will also contribute to Atlantic solidarity and to the establishment of a just and lasting order of peace throughout the whole of Europe.[1]

---

[1] "London Declaration on a Transformed North Atlantic Alliance," London, July 6, 1990 (NATO Press Service, Press Communiqué S-1(90)36), para. 3.

Although the London Declaration acknowledged and welcomed the effort to create a European security identity, it did not attempt to define its nature or role. The focus at London was on the need to revise NATO's military strategy to reflect the reduced threat from the Warsaw Pact.

The breakneck pace of events in the year following the London summit precipitated the need for a more rapid and far-reaching adaptation than NATO leaders had foreseen in mid-1990.[2] At the Copenhagen NATO Ministerial one year later, Germany participated as a newly united country, the Soviet military threat had clearly diminished, and NATO and former Warsaw Pact countries had signed the treaty limiting conventional forces in Europe (CFE Treaty).

At Copenhagen, the Allies accomplished two important tasks: they redefined NATO's role and accelerated the process of developing links with the former Warsaw Pact nations. In a statement on the "Core Security Functions in the New Europe," NATO leaders recast the Alliance's role in contributing to security under changed circumstances. They specified NATO's four key security functions:

(1) To provide one of the indispensable foundations for a stable security environment in Europe, based on the growth of democratic institutions and commitment to the peaceful resolution of disputes, in which no country would be able to intimidate or coerce any European nation or to impose hegemony through the threat or use of force.

(2) To serve, as provided for in Article IV of the North Atlantic Treaty, as a transatlantic forum for Allied consultations on any issues that affect their vital interests, including possible developments posing risks for members' security, and for appropriate coordination of their efforts in fields of common concern.

(3) To deter and defend against any threat of aggression against the territory of any NATO member state.

---

[2]For the history of the evolution of the NATO's new Strategic Concept as it evolved following the London summit, see Michael Legge, "The Making of NATO's New Strategy," *NATO Review*, December 1991, pp. 9–13.

(4)   To preserve the strategic balance within Europe.[3]

Although NATO had always embraced both political and military objectives (a perspective reinforced in the 1967 Harmel Report), this formulation significantly reduced the prominence given to collective defense of Alliance territory. Rather, the Allies emphasized NATO's political role: providing stability and serving as a forum for consultation. Moreover, they stated that the Alliance is *one* of the indispensable foundations for a stable security environment, not the only one. The statement on core security functions acknowledged that other institutions, such as the WEU, also had roles to play in this respect, and that a European security and defense identity would facilitate a larger role for Europeans in providing for their own security. But the statement singled out NATO as pre-eminent: the only institution able to perform all four security functions, and the "essential forum" for Allied consultations and for discussions of commitments under the Washington Treaty.[4]

In the Final Communiqué issued at Copenhagen (accompanying the statement on core security functions), NATO ministers described more specifically their concept for the relationship between the Alliance and EDI and the new role for the Alliance in a transformed Europe. In effect, they spelled out "rules of the road" for creating a new European security architecture. As EC members debated the role of the Community in foreign security policy as part of the ongoing EC intergovernmental conference on political union, the NATO allies welcomed the progress being made toward European unity and the creation of a common foreign and security policy in the context of "the strengthening of the European pillar within the Alliance." They stated that this development would reinforce "the integrity and effectiveness" of the Alliance.[5]

At the same time, they reiterated the Alliance's essential role as a forum for consultation among members on matters affecting security

---

[3]"NATO's Core Security Functions in the New Europe," statement by the North Atlantic Council, Copenhagen, June 7, 1991 (NATO Press Service, Press Communiqué M-1(91)44), para. 6.

[4]Ibid., para. 7.

[5]Final Communiqué, Ministerial Meeting of the North Atlantic Council, Copenhagen, June 7, 1991 (NATO Press Service Press Communiqué M-1(91)40), p. 2.

and defense commitments, and they pledged to enhance that function of the Alliance "in parallel with the emergence and development of a European security identity and defense role."[6] They agreed that NATO and the emerging European security identity should consult closely and coordinate action. Specifically, the Allies agreed that "we will develop practical arrangements to ensure the necessary transparency and complementarity between the European security and defence identity as it emerges in the Twelve and the WEU, and the Alliance."[7]

This formulation implied that smaller groups within NATO (e.g., the EC countries) would not reach agreements in negotiations closed to other Alliance members. But such a pledge could not prevent bilateral consultations or initiatives, which created tensions among the Allies in the context of revising the Alliance's strategic concept as well as in the intra-EC debates over formulating an approach to a European security and defense identity in the European "Union."

This tension intensified in the period between the June 1991 meeting in Copenhagen, NATO's Rome summit in November, and the December meeting at Maastricht to complete negotiations on the Treaty on European Union. EC members of NATO engaged in a vigorous debate over the concept of the European defense identity, driven by the need to frame the European security and defense identity in the context of (1) the Alliance's ongoing work on a revised Strategic Concept and a military reorganization, (2) the EC Intergovernmental Conference on "political union," and (3) a growing interest in the Western European Union as the locus for the defense identity.

The debate crystallized around two alternative concepts: The first, put forth in an Anglo-Italian proposal of October 4, emphasized the role of the European security identity as the European pillar of the Alliance, working through the WEU. The Anglo-Italian Declaration stressed the importance of retaining and strengthening NATO, stating: "The development of a European identity in the field of defence should be construed in such a way as to reinforce the Atlantic

---

[6]Ibid., p. 2.
[7]Ibid., p. 2.

Alliance."[8] The proposal underscored the need for links to NATO as well as the EC, and focused on complementing NATO, primarily for out-of-area operations, leaving NATO sole responsibility for defending Allied territory. The declaration proposed creating a "Europe Reaction Force" consisting of forces separate from the NATO structure and designed specifically for responses "outside the NATO area."[9] Denmark, the Netherlands, and Portugal, members of the Alliance who questioned the desirability of an independent defense component to the European Union, supported this approach.

The second alternative was embodied in a Franco-German proposal of October 14, which asserted that a true European Union must include a full range of responsibilities for foreign policy and defense. In addition to spelling out in detail their ideas for implementing a common foreign and security policy, Chancellor Kohl and President Mitterrand sketched out an approach to security that would eventually lead the European Community to assume responsibility for defending its members, independent of (but consistent with) NATO.

SETTING THE AGENDA: ROME AND MAASTRICHT

At its Rome summit in November 1991, the Alliance reaffirmed its previously adopted approach and elaborated in greater detail the framework for a new security architecture. In the months after Copenhagen, the international context continued to change dramatically. Following the abortive coup in Moscow in August, the former adversary was not merely less threatening, it was on the verge of disappearing altogether. NATO countries broadly accepted the need for more radical changes in the structure of European security.

Although Alliance leaders took pains to stress NATO's essential role, they recognized that NATO alone—even with a revised strategy—could not meet all the security needs of the new strategic setting and that other institutions would play enlarged roles in the new Europe. In the "Rome Declaration on Peace and Cooperation," the heads of state and government asserted that "we are working toward a new

---

[8]"Declaration on European Security and Defence," October 4, 1991 (New York: British Information Services, Policy Statement 62/91), p. 2.

[9]Ibid., p. 3.

European security architecture in which NATO, the CSCE, the European Community, the WEU, and the Council of Europe complement each other." They hoped to achieve this complementarity through "a framework of interlocking institutions tying together the countries of Europe and North America."[10]

The concept of "interlocking" institutions implied more than close relationships. It also suggested the need to establish formal linkages, echoing the commitment originally announced at Copenhagen, to "develop practical arrangements to ensure the necessary transparency and complementarity between the European security and defence identity as it emerges in the Twelve and the WEU, and the Alliance."[11]

NATO also formally acknowledged that the WEU would play an important role in the development of the European defense identity, not limited simply to a strengthened European pillar of the Atlantic Alliance. Specifically, NATO "welcomed" the WEU's enhanced role, "both as the defence component of the process of European unification and as a means of strengthening the European pillar of the Alliance, bearing in mind the different nature of its relations with the Alliance and with the European Political Union."[12]

At Rome the Alliance also adopted a new Strategic Concept based on the four core functions of the Alliance originally spelled out at Copenhagen. The Alliance explicitly welcomed the creation of a European security and defense identity, noting that it "will underline the preparedness of the Europeans to take a greater share of responsibility for their security and will help to reinforce transatlantic solidarity."[13] The Strategic Concept also reiterated NATO members' commitments on "transparency and complementarity between the European security and defense identity and the Alliance."[14]

---

[10]"Rome Declaration on Peace and Cooperation," Rome, November 8, 1991 (NATO Press Service, Press Communiqué S-1(91)86), para. 3.

[11]Ibid., para. 6.

[12]Ibid., para. 7.

[13]"The Alliance's New Strategic Concept," Rome, November 7, 1991 (NATO Press Service, Press Communiqué S-1(91)85), para. 22.

[14]Ibid., para. 52.

The Alliance reaffirmed the importance of the NATO integrated military command. But, in a key phrase in the same paragraph, the leaders also acknowledged that integration need not occur only in NATO:

> Integrated and multinational European structures, as they are further developed in the context of an emerging European Defence Identity, will also increasingly have a similarly important role to play in enhancing the Allies' ability to work together in the common defence.[15]

The ambiguity of this formulation, included as a concession to France, caused considerable difficulty in the controversy surrounding the creation of a Franco-German Corps.

Over the course of the seventeen months between the London and Rome summits, NATO thus reached an apparent consensus on the need for, and role of, a European security identity. It remained for the Europeans to agree among themselves how to realize and structure it. These issues were addressed in the context of the Treaty on European Union, agreed at Maastricht, the Netherlands, in December 1991 and signed in February 1992.

At Maastricht, EC members were concerned with a broad range of issues relating to European integration, including a common foreign and security policy, and a future defense identity.[16] The Treaty on European Union does not refer explicitly to a defense "identity." Instead, it commits the Twelve to a common foreign and security policy leading to "the eventual framing of a common defence policy which might in time lead to a common defence."[17] The treaty agreed to at Maastricht also declares the WEU to be "an integral part of the development of the Union," and asks the WEU to "elaborate and

---

[15]Ibid., para. 52.

[16]For a more extensive discussion of the debate over common foreign and security policy and defense leading up to the Maastricht decision, see James B. Steinberg, *An Ever Closer Union: European Integration and its Implications for the Future of U.S.-European Relations*, Santa Monica, CA: RAND, R-4177-A, 1992.

[17]Treaty on European Union, Article J.4.1 (Luxembourg, Office for Official Publications of the European Communities), 1992, p. 126.

implement decisions and actions of the Union which have defence implications."[18]

At Maastricht, the nine members of the WEU issued a parallel declaration to accompany the treaty, agreeing on "the need to develop a genuine European security and defense identity and a greater European responsibility on defense matters."[19] The declaration reiterated the WEU's two roles—as a defense component of the European Union and the means to strengthen the European pillar of NATO—and it outlined concrete steps to build the two linkages. The declaration also identified measures to strengthen the WEU's operational role, including forming a planning cell; military cooperation "complementary to the Alliance" on logistics, transport, training, and strategic surveillance; and military units answerable to the WEU. In a separate declaration, the WEU members set out a framework for relations with European states that belong to either the EC or NATO, but not the WEU. EC members were invited to become full members of the WEU (or observers, if they so choose), while European NATO members were invited to become associate WEU members "in a way which will give them the possibility of participating fully in the activities of the WEU."[20]

In practice, however, neither Rome nor Maastricht definitively resolved the debate over EDI, as the months following the Maastricht summit rapidly made clear. The Maastricht declarations did, however, provide a framework for the subsequent efforts to create an operational European defense identity. As West European governments moved from defining the concept of European defense identity to giving it operational form, they faced practical as well as political challenges. These are discussed in the next chapter.

---

[18]Ibid., Article J.4.2, p. 126.

[19]*Declaration on the Role of the Western European Union and its Relations with the European Union and with the Atlantic Alliance,* Maastricht, December 10, 1991, para. 2 (hereinafter cited as WEU Maastricht Declaration I).

[20]"Declaration by Belgium, Germany, Spain, France, Italy, Luxembourg, the Netherlands, Portugal and the United Kingdom of Great Britain and Northern Ireland which are members of the Western European Union," Maastricht, December 10, 1991 (hereinafter, WEU Maastricht Declaration II).

Chapter Three

ORGANIZING THE EUROPEAN DEFENSE IDENTITY: THE FRANCO-GERMAN CORPS AND THE WESTERN EUROPEAN UNION

As European governments proposed concrete measures to implement the goal of a European defense identity, differences in concept and approach emerged. These debates were complicated by shifting currents in domestic politics and crises of political leadership, by regional and national elections in several key countries, and by Danish voters' rejection of the Maastricht Treaty in a June 1992 referendum. Amid the political turbulence and the rapid pace of external events, Europeans continued to struggle over two alternative concepts of EDI: the defense expression of the European Union, or the European pillar of the Atlantic Alliance.

Although there is no a priori conflict between the twin objectives of strengthening the European pillar of the Atlantic Alliance and creating a defense component of the Union, at times the polemics of the debate appeared to present them as either/or alternatives. The fundamental issue that preoccupied members of the European Community was the relative emphasis or priority to be given to each. The compromise at Maastricht proved fragile, not only because the leaders left many important questions unsettled, but also because they were tempted to relitigate the balance that Maastricht appeared to strike.

The European debate during most of 1992 revolved around eight central questions:

(1) Should the EDI limit its activities to operations out of the "NATO area," or should it also play a role in territorial defense?

(2)   Should the EDI include creating standing European peacetime forces and a separate European command structure?

(3)   Should the forces of the EDI be capable of operating autonomously outside the traditional NATO area, even at the cost of duplicating NATO assets?

(4)   Will the forces be available for internationally sponsored missions, such as peacekeeping or peacemaking?

(5)   Should the WEU remain independent, or merge into the EC?

(6)   How should EC and NATO members that are not members of the WEU participate in WEU activities?

(7)   Where there is a conflict between NATO and WEU/European missions, should NATO or the WEU have priority in terms of political decisionmaking and command responsibility?

(8)   Should all European forces be subordinate to the WEU for non-NATO activities, or should other structures (such as the Franco-German Corps) maintain operational independence?

As Table 1 shows, the Alliance's four principal military powers differed over these issues, with the most wide-ranging disagreements between France and the United Kingdom (supported by the United States). Germany's position, although politically allied with France

Table 1

Views of the Emerging EDI in 1992

	France	Germany	United Kingdom	United States
In-area	+	+	—	—
Standing forces in peacetime	+	?	—	—
Autonomous outside NATO	+	—	+	—
Peacekeeping	+	+	+	+
Merged into EC	+	+	—	—
Full participation by non-WEU members	—	?	+	+
NATO priority	—	?	+	+
WEU controls European forces	—	?	+	+

in a series of Franco-German initiatives, was more ambivalent for two reasons: Germany did not want to jeopardize its strong ties with the United States, and the ongoing German domestic debate over whether to permit the use of German forces outside the NATO area and outside the NATO framework made it difficult for German leaders to adopt clear-cut positions.

These conceptual differences crystallized around two competing proposals for developing the European defense identity: the Franco-German Corps as the "core" or model for European defense cooperation, and the British proposal for developing the Western European Union as the organizing institution.

THE FRANCO-GERMAN CORPS ("EUROCORPS")

Background: The Kohl-Mitterrand Proposal

Beginning with their joint letter to the Irish Presidency of the EC in April 1990, Chancellor Helmut Kohl of Germany and President François Mitterrand of France had pushed for expanding the EC's role in European foreign policy and defense. As the Maastricht summit approached, they fleshed out their ideas in a letter to the prime minister of the Netherlands, Ruud Lubbers, in his role as Chairman of the European Council of Ministers, on October 14, 1991.[1] The letter focused principally on the evolution of the CFSP and on the role of the WEU and its relationship with the European Union. In what appears almost as an afterthought, Kohl and Mitterrand appended to their letter a "note" announcing the proposed "initiative":

> Franco-German military cooperation will be reinforced beyond the existing brigade. The reinforced Franco-German units could thus become the nucleus [noyau] of a European corps which could include the forces of other WEU member states. This new structure could also become the model for closer military cooperation among WEU member states.[2]

---

[1] "The Franco-German Initiative on the European Foreign and Security Policy," *Le Monde*, October 17, 1991, p. 4.

[2] Ibid. (author's translation).

This cryptic reference launched what would prove to be an intensive fourteen months of discussions and heated debate among West European states and between Europe and the United States.

The initial proposal was rife with ambiguity. Although added as a note to a letter focused primarily on the WEU's role in building a defense identity to augment the European Union, the proposal failed to specify how the Corps would relate to the WEU; other WEU members are simply identified as potential contributors to the Corps. The Corps is described as a "model" for cooperation among the nine WEU members, suggesting that perhaps the Corps itself would operate independent of the WEU. By raising the implication that the founders intended to create a separate entity outside the WEU or any other security structure, the proposal created suspicions among other Europeans and in the United States. Some observers viewed it as the nucleus of a true "European army," some as the principal WEU-based force, some as the beginning of an organization to rival NATO.[3]

Since the approach emphasized developing the defense dimension of the European Union, rather than strengthening the "European Pillar" of the Alliance, a number of allies worried about overlap between missions for the proposed Eurocorps and those currently performed by NATO.[4] This concern was reinforced by an awareness that, in the prevailing German political climate, there was no consensus in favor of assigning German forces to any mission other than in the NATO area.

The two leaders themselves provided the main impetus for including the idea of the Corps in the proposal; it was clearly not elaborately staffed or negotiated between the two governments. Defense ministries in each country had little, if any, involvement in formulating the idea and showed little enthusiasm for it. When Germany's Defense Minister Stoltenberg attempted to explain the concept to his

---

[3]Since early in 1991, French policy had been moving away from emphasizing the WEU as a "bridge" to NATO and toward the development of an independent European defense. See "In the beginning was the word, and the word was defence," *The Economist*, May 24, 1991, p. 59.

[4]See "NATO unease on Franco-German plan," *The Independent*, October 22, 1991, p. 12, and "NATO's Outlook Clouded by French-German Plan," *Washington Post*, October 19, 1991, p. 20.

NATO colleagues at the Alliance's Nuclear Planning Group meeting shortly after the letter was released, his efforts were, according to published accounts, unsatisfying.[5]

Because the initial proposal for the Corps contained few details, it remained for the bureaucracies of the two countries to work out its concrete aspects in subsequent discussions. A number of European countries, such as Belgium and Spain, expressed interest in participating in the Corps. Germany and France held seminars in early 1992 to outline the proposal further and to attract additional participation. Following the meetings, however, no additional partners signed on to the Eurocorps. According to some accounts, neither France nor Germany made a serious effort to involve other countries in the Corps' design or to identify meaningful roles for additional participants. Many fellow WEU members, especially the United Kingdom and Italy, expressed resentment at the bilateral effort. They regarded it as inconsistent with the Maastricht pledge to act at the level of the nine WEU nations and with commitments to "transparency and complementarity" made to NATO.[6]

Sources of the Proposal

The proposed Eurocorps had its roots in several longstanding, broadly held policy goals of the two countries. But their objectives were not identical, and these differences led each to articulate somewhat divergent views on the Corps' nature and operational role.

For most of the post–World War II era, French policy had focused on developing close Franco-German political, economic, and security ties as a means of preventing a renewal of hostility between the two countries. From the days of the Pleven plan for a common European foreign policy in the early 1950s, through the Fouchet proposals for a European political union in 1960, and the Elysée Treaty of 1963, French leaders sought to strengthen the Franco-German link, either multilaterally or bilaterally. After a period of relative inattention, this strategy received new emphasis with the 1986 decision to "revive"

---

[5]"U.S. Wary of European Corps, Seeks Assurance on NATO Role," *The New York Times*, October 20, 1991, p. 12.

[6]Interviews in Europe, March 1992.

the Elysée Treaty, and the creation (in 1988) of the joint Franco-German Defense and Security Council, along with the decision to establish a joint Franco-German brigade.

The end of the Cold War and German unification gave new urgency to this strategy from the French perspective. Faced with a larger, more powerful Germany, France was eager to assure that Germany did not pursue an independent course in the new political environment. For French leaders, the need to integrate Germany was especially urgent, given their conviction that American withdrawal from Europe was imminent with the end of the Cold War.

Germany had its own reasons for pursuing the Franco-German initiative. Since the days of Chancellor Adenauer, the commitment to close Franco-German relations (as the core of wider European integration) formed a cornerstone of German policy, driven by a belief that stability in Europe (to say nothing of German unity) depended on permanent Franco-German rapprochement. In German eyes, this approach was the only acceptable path to "normalize" its foreign policy and play a more active international role without creating a perception that Germany might threaten its neighbors.[7] Chancellor Kohl in particular placed heavy emphasis on Franco-German cooperation to reassure its European partners as part of gaining international support for German unification.

The specific Franco-German proposal was, in part, a response to the Anglo-Italian alternative formulation for an EDI offered earlier in October. France and Germany, which had acted as the "motor" of European integration throughout the Intergovernmental Conference on Political Union, sought to regain the initiative in the weeks leading up to the final negotiations over the Maastricht Treaty by proposing their own vision of EDI.

The Anglo-Italian proposal, which retained the WEU's separate identity outside the EC, was at variance with France's core conviction that a European Union required a common, EC-centered defense. Drawing on both the success and limits of U.S.-European cooperation in the 1992 Gulf War, the Anglo-Italian proposal also empha-

---

[7]See Ronald D. Asmus, *German Unification and Its Ramifications*, Santa Monica, CA: RAND, R-4041-A, 1991.

sized the need to strengthen Europe's ability to act as the U.S. military partner, while leaving common territorial defense to existing NATO structures. For France, it was unacceptable that EDI be denied a role in territorial defense, while Germany could not accept an out-of-area role. Thus for both partners, the Anglo-Italian approach was seriously flawed.

The Corps also helped President Mitterrand resolve a practical problem concerning the future stationing of French troops on German territory. In response to German unification, Mitterrand announced, over German objections, plans to withdraw France's military forces from Germany, apparently in the belief that the end to Germany's occupied status removed the rationale for stationing foreign troops there. Over time, Mitterrand appears to have decided that this step was precipitous and counterproductive. The Corps offered a face-saving way to keep French troops on German soil by providing a new basis for their continued presence linked not to the World War II occupation but to the new collaborative relationship. The idea of the Corps appealed to Germany for similar reasons, providing new legitimacy for maintaining the French presence as well as providing "symmetry" by opening up the possibility of stationing German troops (at least staff officers) in France as part of the Corps headquarters.

German and French dissatisfaction over NATO's establishment of the Allied Command Europe Rapid Reaction Corps (ARRC) also contributed to the decision to launch the Eurocorps. The ARRC was designed as NATO's principal military tool for short-notice contingencies. In developing the ARRC's structure, U.S. and NATO authorities accepted Britain's arguments that the future of a continued British troop presence on the Continent depended on giving Britain command of the ARRC. Many German military and civilian leaders believed that the size of the German military contribution to the ARRC and its presence on German soil argued for German command, and they resented what they perceived as indifference to Germany's legitimate claims.[8]

---

[8]This view was repeatedly expressed by officials in Bonn and London as well as by NATO officials during interviews in March 1992. Subsequently, as the NATO command structure has taken form and German officers have assumed increasingly important roles, much of this bitterness seems to have dissipated.

Germany's critical view of the ARRC meshed well with France's attitude. French leaders had vehemently criticized NATO's decision to create the ARRC, on the grounds that NATO was prematurely deciding on force structure before it had defined its future strategic concept. Underlying France's hostility to the ARRC was its fear that the ARRC would form the basis for future NATO operations outside the NATO area, thus broadening the area of NATO responsibility and indirectly expanding U.S. influence at the expense of the European Union or other security institutions.

The United States, as well as the Atlanticist members of the WEU, greeted the Eurocorps' launch skeptically, fearing that Germany had fallen into a French "trap" to destroy NATO. Germany faced a difficult balancing act: the desire to harmonize Franco-German relations without at the same time damaging the NATO Alliance or Germany's transatlantic ties. In the same month that the Franco-German Corps was proposed, German Foreign Minister Genscher and U.S. Secretary of State Baker announced a proposal for creating the North Atlantic Cooperation Council (NACC), a forum associated with NATO to foster dialogue with the former Warsaw Pact adversaries. The move, broadening NATO's political role in the post–Cold War era, was not well received in Paris, which viewed NACC as a thinly disguised effort to preserve U.S. political dominance in Europe. The German embrace of NACC could be seen as a kind of compensation to the United States for the Eurocorps, which some in the United States viewed as anti-NATO.

Structure of the Franco-German Corps

Six months of negotiations and planning for the Corps culminated in the Franco-German summit on May 21, 1992, at La Rochelle, France, where President Mitterrand and Chancellor Kohl reached final agreement on establishing the Eurocorps. While the two sides had worked out most of the points in advance, some final discussions by the two leaders were required to complete the arrangement, further demonstrating the high-level political involvement that animated the Corps' creation.[9]

---

[9]The broad outlines of the Corps' structure were agreed upon as early as March (interviews in Paris, Bonn, and Brussels, March 1992). The two leaders were clearly

The two governments agreed to establish a Joint Committee to coordinate policies and to direct the Corps. The existing German-French Council on Defense and Security will assume the responsibilities of the Joint Committee until other WEU member states decide to join the Eurocorps. This Committee is also responsible for relations with other relevant security organizations, such as NATO or the WEU.

A key issue is the peacetime authority of the Corps' Commanding General over forces assigned to the Corps. According to paragraph B.2.2.1 of the La Rochelle agreement, the Commanding General has responsibility for operational and logistics planning, contributing to setting training goals, monitoring readiness, preparing and conducting exercises, and making other proposals as necessary, e.g., concerning the organization of the forces. In order to carry out these responsibilities, the Commanding General must first submit his recommendations to the Joint Committee and receive instructions from the Committee and the national authorities.[10] For matters of pay and individual discipline, national authorities retain jurisdiction.[11] Moreover, it would appear that "peacetime command" is primarily national. According to paragraph B.2.2 of the La Rochelle agreement,

> The formations are primarily subordinated to the Corps and are intended for joint missions. In the absence of an operational mission, the formations subordinated to the Corps will remain in all respects under national command without prejudice to the competence of the Commanding General of the European Corps.[12]

---

the primary actors pushing the establishment of the Corps; the defense establishments and, to a lesser degree, the foreign ministries were less enthusiastic. Moreover, in Germany the opposition Social Democratic Party was noticeably reticent in its support, and some parliamentarians were openly critical of the idea.

[10]"Report of the German and French Defense Ministers on the Creation of the European Corps," adopted May 22, 1992, by the German-French Council on Defense and Security, para. B.2.2.1. Hereafter cited as La Rochelle Report.

[11]This conclusion is consistent with a subsequent French description of the Corps' organization. See *Le Monde*, May 7, 1993, p. 13, "La France Précise l'Organisation du Commandant et les Missions propos au corps européen." The article draws on an article in a French Ministry of Defense publication, *Objective Defense* (Spring 1993), entitled "L'avènement du corps européen."

[12]La Rochelle Report, para. B.2.2.

Despite this rather explicit indication that national authorities retain command of the forces "in the absence of an operational mission," the French argued that the forces subordinated to the Corps are under the peacetime command of the Commanding General of the Corps. Germany, however, argues that its forces are "dual-hatted," committed to NATO as well as to the Corps. Consequently, during peacetime the forces would remain under German national command.[13]   If, for example, the Commanding General of the Corps wanted to conduct an exercise he could request permission through the Joint Committee, but the option of participating would remain within the German national command's sphere of competence. Should either national authority wish to use the assigned forces outside the Corps structure, it need only go through an "informational procedure" (yet to be specified) to the Joint Committee.

The use of the Joint Committee as the center of political responsibility for the Corps contains further elements of ambiguity, since the committee's specific functions and operating rules are not spelled out. Such ambiguities could discourage other countries from contributing troops to the Corps, since it is unclear how other participants would be represented on this committee, an issue now under negotiation in the context of Belgium's decision in spring 1993 to join the Corps. If the Corps expands in size and membership, its supporting organizations and structures would likewise expand, potentially complicating its relationship to the constituent governments, to the WEU, and to NATO.

The Planning Staff became operational on July 1, 1992, tasked first with planning and establishing the Corps Headquarters in Strasbourg by June 1993. As of the summer of 1993, some 300 French and

---

[13]See "French and Germans Plan an Army Corps Despite NATO Fears," *The New York Times*, May 23, 1992, p. 1: "France and Germany also have different interpretations of the Corps' peacetime role, with Paris arguing that its division and Germany's two brigades should be assigned exclusively to the Corps and Bonn insisting that its forces will be 'double-hatted' and will answer first to NATO." According to some German officials, the La Rochelle language is intentionally vague, enabling each side to present its own interpretation. One German official explained (in an interview in March 1992) that there would be no explicit reference to "dual-hatting" because a "more artful formulation" had been used.

German officers were posted to Strasbourg.[14] The first Commanding General, General Helmut Willmann of Germany, will assume command in October 1993, when the first troops become available to the Corps (the French-German brigade as well as other troops). Deputy Commanders will represent all other participating countries. The Corps Headquarters will be fully operational by July 1994.[15] The Corps itself is scheduled to be formed and completely operational by October 1, 1995. The two countries have not finally decided which units they will contribute to the Corps, but according to a French Defense Ministry document, the French contribution will include the 1st Armored Division (stationed in Baden, Germany), the 42nd Signals Regiment, and the 10th Engineer Regiment. The article suggests that Germany might designate its 12th and 30th mechanized brigades, as well as staff elements from the 10th Panzer division.[16] Only the staff will be multinational; operational units (other than the Franco-German brigade) will remain under national rules and national supervision. The Corps itself is primarily a land force, but the two countries have agreed to make available air and naval assets as needed.[17]

Roles

The communiqué issued at La Rochelle specifically enumerated the tasks of the Corps:

(1) Joint defense of allied territory, under the Brussels or Washington treaties;

(2) Peacekeeping ("maintaining or reestablishing peace");

(3) Humanitarian missions.[18]

---

[14]See *Le Monde,* May 7, 1993, p. 131; Europe 1 Radio, May 21, 1993, in FBIS-WEU-93-097, May 21, 1993, p. 33.

[15]La Rochelle Report, para. B.2.2.2.

[16]*Le Monde,* May 7, 1993; "L'avènement du corps européen," op. cit.

[17]Ibid.

[18]La Rochelle Report, para. B.1.1. Humanitarian missions include catastrophic assistance, famine relief, refugee aid, and evacuations from crisis regions. See also "L'avènement du corps européen," op. cit., p. 3.

These role definitions are highly general. It is unclear whether France and Germany intend to structure and equip the Corps around these highly diverse missions, or whether they intend a "division of labor" between national units and the Corps. Since it will be composed of relatively heavy forces and does not appear likely to have much mobility, the Corps would seem a poor candidate for use outside the territory of the two countries, even if Germany reaches a new political consensus allowing German forces to perform those missions. However, the recent French MoD description of the Corps plays down the importance of structure as such, describing the forces committed to the Corps as a "reservoir" from which the headquarters can create operational groupings using a task-force approach to tailor forces to the mission in question. The existing Franco-German Brigade will be a part of the new Corps, although its role is unclear as well.[19]

Relationship of the Franco-German Corps to Existing Security Structures

The Corps' founding document echoes the French view linking the future European defense identity to the European Union:

> The European Corps is to allow Europe to have its own means for military action at its disposal. By its creation the states participating in the European Corps manifest their intent to jointly fulfill their responsibility in the area of security and the preservation of peace within the framework of a European Union, which in the long run will also involve a joint defense policy.[20]

At the same time, both Kohl and Mitterrand took care to describe the effort as complementary to NATO, declaring in a joint statement that the Corps "will contribute to strengthening the Atlantic Alliance."[21] Kohl, perhaps reflecting the internal tensions in the German posi-

---

[19]*Le Monde*, May 23–24, 1993, p. 8. The ability of the Franco-German brigade to conduct humanitarian missions is to be established by January, 1994. La Rochelle Report, Part C.

[20]La Rochelle Report, para B.1.

[21]"French and Germans Plan an Army Corps Despite NATO Fears," *The New York Times*, May 23, 1992, p. 1.

tion, declared that the Corps was an "extension of NATO," and also "a step on the way to a European defense identity."[22]   Defense Minister Rühe, also speaking at La Rochelle, declared: "We have clearly indicated that the commitments to other defence organizations will not be affected. This is important for Germany but also for other countries which may be interested in joining the Eurocorps."[23]

Both Kohl and Mitterrand also attempted to deflect American criticism of the Corps by arguing that the United States had long encouraged the Europeans to assume a greater share of their own defense, and should therefore welcome this development.[24]   At La Rochelle, Kohl stated: "The Americans often tell us we should do more for our own security . . . This Corps should be a reason to celebrate in Washington, because Europeans are finally doing what they have been asked to do for a long time."[25]   Mitterrand echoed the same theme a few weeks later, stating that "I can see nothing in this initiative that could overshadow the Atlantic alliance . . . This is our aim: to help strengthen joint security and to revitalize the alliance, creating a true partnership between the two sides of the Atlantic."[26]

The La Rochelle communiqué delegates specific responsibilities for relations to existing security structures to the Joint Committee. In addition to the functions for oversight of the Corps described above, the committee is also given the task (in paragraph B.2.1) of coordinating relations with NATO, the WEU, and other international organizations. The committee's structure is also directed to be "as compatible as possible with the structures presently being worked out within the WEU."   The exact nature of the role to be played by the Joint Committee and, in particular, its relationship to NATO and the WEU, was not clearly spelled out. Some critics of the concept raised the question of why two NATO and WEU members needed to form a

---

[22]"Kohl, Mitterrand Reject Criticism," Hamburg DPA, May 22, 1992, in FBIS-WEU-92-101, May 26, 1992, p. 5.

[23]"Opposition to Force Noted," Agence France Presse, May 22, 1992, in FBIS-WEU-92-101, May 26, 1992, p. 6.

[24]"U.S., Bonn Clash over Pact with France," *Wall Street Journal*, May 27, 1992, p. A11.

[25]"France, Germany Unveil Corps as Step Toward European Defense," *Washington Post*, May 23, 1991.

[26]"Mitterrand on EC Consolidation, Enlargement," *Expresso* (Lisbon), June 27, 1992, in FBIS-WEU-92-137, July 16, 1992, p. 2.

separate committee for purposes of discussions with NATO or the WEU.

The debate over the Corps' relationship to NATO focused on two issues: *when* and *how* the Corps would operate within the NATO framework. The *when* issue arose because, at least for territorial defense, both NATO and the Corps have similar missions, and the areas of overlap are likely to grow as NATO extends its role out of area. The *how* issue arose because France sought to reinforce the idea of the Corps as a unit, which would fight as a unit, rather than an umbrella for loosely connected forces that could fight together or separately.

Although both Kohl and Mitterrand stressed the compatibility between the Corps and NATO, the La Rochelle communiqué raised difficult questions concerning who decides the priority of missions and operational use of the forces assigned to the Corps. Paragraph B.3.2.2 stated that future agreements to be worked out at the political and operational levels between NATO and the Corps will establish the terms under which the Corps would be available for the NATO main defense mission under Article 5 of the Washington Treaty. "The purpose of these agreements," according to the key sentence of the paragraph, "is to clearly establish the priority of the use of the Corps as a European Corps."

While France consistently sought to retain the Corps' organizational identity as a unit, even when it comes under NATO operational control, this approach raised uncertainties concerning the German forces' independent assignment to NATO missions. Subsequent statements from Paris and Bonn appeared to indicate that the Eurocorps would be placed under SACEUR in the event the Corps were to participate in defense of NATO territory.[27] The effectiveness of this force in performing the main NATO defense mission without participating (as a Corps) in NATO's integrated command or prior planning process could have been in doubt, although for French forces in the Corps this represented virtually no change from existing policy.

---

[27]The strongest statement on this point is probably that of Pierre Joxe, French defense minister, who is quoted as observing: "In the event of aggression, the European corps will, of course, operate under the authority of a NATO commander. That has already been decided." "Joxe's Vision of a Euro Army," *Jane's Defence Weekly*, June, 20, 1992, p. 1074.

German officials responded to this criticism by arguing that since the first mission of the Corps is territorial defense and since the German troops assigned to NATO would also be involved in such a defense, there is no reason to see German participation in the Corps as weakening Germany's commitment to participate fully in NATO. Indeed, German officials argued that by getting France to agree to participate in the Corps, Germany succeeded in drawing France closer to the Alliance. But this argument does not address the problem created by France's apparent insistence that the Corps fight "as a corps," since the German troops are assigned NATO missions without regard to the Eurocorps. Absent a more formal linkage between the planning systems and forces of the Corps and SHAPE (Supreme Headquarters Allied Powers Europe), the German argument that France is being drawn closer to NATO would simply gloss over a real ambiguity in the direction of German policy.

At NATO's spring 1992 ministerial meetings, neither the Defense Planning Committee nor the North Atlantic Council referred specifically to the La Rochelle announcement. In an oblique reference, the DPC "stressed the importance of maintaining existing assignments to NATO of forces being considered for use by the WEU, recognizing that the primary responsibility of these forces is to meet the collective defence commitments of the Alliance, under the terms of the Washington Treaty."[28] One week later, NATO's Foreign Ministers issued a similar cautionary statement: "As the transformation of the Alliance proceeds, we intend to preserve the operational coherence we now have and on which our defence depends. We stress the importance of maintaining Allies' existing obligations and commitments of forces to NATO." The ministers also restated that the primary responsibility of forces answerable to the WEU remained NATO territorial defense.[29]

During the course of the summer and autumn of 1992, French and German officials searched for a formula that would assure the bilateral and European goals of the Corps, while meeting the standards

---

[28]Final Communiqué, Defence Planning Committee and Nuclear Planning Group, Press Communiqué M-DPC/NPG-1(92)44, May 27, 1992, para. 6.

[29]Final Communiqué, Ministerial Meeting of the North Atlantic Council in Oslo, Norway, Press Communiqué M-NAC-1(92)51, June 4, 1992, para. 7.

laid down by NATO. This effort bore fruit in a bilateral understanding in November that led to negotiations with SACEUR in December.[30] These talks quickly resulted in a formal agreement between the French and German defense chiefs, Admiral Jacques Lanxade and General Klaus Naumann, and SACEUR, which was approved by NATO's Military Committee on December 22, 1992.[31] The agreement was formally initialed by the three military leaders on January 21, 1993.[32]

Given the rather heated exchanges surrounding the original announcement of the Corps in October 1992, the agreement was reached with relative ease. In part this reflected evolving French attitudes toward NATO, which had moved away from somewhat rigid assertions of French independence to more practical forms of accommodation.[33] NATO leaders, too, had grown to see that the Eurocorps might strengthen, rather than weaken, NATO's capability. In a statement issued just before France, Germany, and NATO reached final agreement, the DPC ministers "welcomed . . . the initiative of France and Germany to establish a European Corps that is intended to be available for Alliance missions and thus to provide a significant contribution to strengthening the European pillar of the Alliance."[34]

Both sides could point to features of the agreement that reflected key objectives. From NATO's point of view, the agreement satisfactorily addressed the Alliance's two major concerns: the command relationship between NATO and the Corps, and the status of NATO-

---

[30]See "Eurocorps to be Subordinated to NATO," *Süddeutsche Zeitung,* November 19, 1992, p. 7, in FBIS-WEU-92-233, December 3, 1992, p. 1; David Buchan, "Paris Agrees on NATO Role in Eurocorps," *Financial Times,* December 1, 1992.

[31]"Initiative by France and Germany for a European Corps," NATO Press Service, Press Release (2)111, December 22, 1992. Also see "Signing of Agreement on the Eurocorps," *Atlantic News,* January 15, 1993.

[32]David Buchan, "NATO Blessing for the Eurocorps," *Financial Times,* January 22, 1993, p. 2.

[33]The new attitude was evident in several speeches by the former defense minister under the Socialist government, Pierre Joxe, and has continued under his successor, François Léotard. See, e.g., Joxe's speech at the annual Wehrkunde conference in Germany, *Le Figaro,* February 8, 1993, p. 11.

[34]Final Communiqué, Defense Planning Committee, Brussels, December 11, 1992 (NATO Press Service, Press Communiqué M-DPC-2(92)102), p. 3.

assigned German troops also assigned to the Corps. France (along with Germany) agreed to place the Eurocorps under NATO operational command not only for collective defense, under Article 5 of the Washington Treaty, but also potentially for NATO operations, such as peacekeeping, beyond NATO territory.[35] While previous, unpublicized agreements between France and NATO established procedures for bringing French forces under NATO's operational *control* in time of war, the agreement represents the first time since 1966 that France has accepted (at least in principle), the idea of NATO operational *command* of French forces. This new arrangement gives SACEUR greater freedom to determine both the missions and the command arrangements governing the Eurocorps' use under Article 5, though continuing to preserve France's authority over whether to commit troops in the first instance. The agreement also preserved the German troops' "dual-hatting"; they would continue to receive NATO assignments as part of NATO integrated command in addition to their role in the Eurocorps.

France, in turn, achieved several key objectives. First, both France and Germany must agree in advance before the Eurocorps can come under NATO command.[36] Second, the Eurocorps would come under NATO command as an entity (*en tant que tel*); NATO commanders would not be free to deploy the Corps' constituent units separately. Finally, the Corps would retain its freedom to act in non-NATO contingencies.

Less clear from the press accounts and other commentary surrounding the announcement of the agreement is the Eurocorps' relationship to NATO in those contingencies not involving direct defense of NATO territory. Although both Paris and Bonn contended from the Corps' inception that it would be available for peacekeeping and other operations, the insistence by the French in late 1992 and early

---

[35]The actual agreement between France, Germany, and NATO remains classified. The description here is drawn from public statements by NATO and government officials and from press accounts. See David Buchan, "Paris Agrees on NATO role in Eurocorps," *Financial Times*, January 22, 1993, p. 2; Daniel Vernet, "Paris Takes Another Step Toward NATO," *Le Monde*, March 12, 1993, pp. 1, 6; and "L'avènement du corps européen," op. cit.

[36]The nations participating in the Eurocorps retain the authority over whether to make it available to NATO in the context of collective defense under Article 5 of the Washington Treaty.

1993 that any military operations in former Yugoslavia be under United Nations rather than NATO auspices suggests that the French are not yet prepared to see NATO act as an alliance in out-of-area contingencies or peacekeeping operations. In practice, however, once asked by the United Nations to act, NATO command arrange-' ments are likely to be used, and the distinctions insistently maintained in political discussions may prove largely irrelevant to the military operations themselves. This can be seen in France's participation in enforcing the no-fly zone over Bosnia, which is conducted through NATO command structures under Security Council mandate, as well as the agreement to form a single command for the NATO and WEU ships in the Adriatic.

The NATO-Eurocorps agreement paved the way for Belgium to announce its intention to participate in the Corps. Belgium decided to dual-hat its mechanized division with Eurocorps and NATO main defense force assignments (similar to the arrangement for German troops in the Eurocorps), while the Belgian paratroop brigade retains only a NATO Rapid Reaction Force assignment.[37]   Spain has also informally indicated that it will participate in the Corps, most likely beginning in 1994.

THE WESTERN EUROPEAN UNION

On paper, the two Maastricht agreements established a rather detailed framework for developing the Western European Union in its two dimensions: as the strengthened European pillar within the Alliance, and as the expression of the European defense identity. But in reality Maastricht was more a cease-fire between the two contending concepts than a durable agreement, and a host of unresolved issues lay beneath the language of the Maastricht documents.

The WEU Declaration issued in conjunction with the Treaty on European Union at Maastricht linked the WEU to the Community's common foreign and security policy and elaborated the dual roles the WEU would undertake:

---

[37]See *Le Monde*, May 14, 1993, p. 5; *Le Soir* (Brussels), April 15, 1993, p. 4.

> WEU will be developed as the defence component of the European Union and as a means to strengthen the European pillar of the Atlantic Alliance. To this end, it will formulate common European defence policy and carry forward its concrete implementation through the further development of its own operational role.[38]

As preliminary steps in developing the operational role, the WEU leaders announced that they would create a planning cell, identify military units answerable to the WEU, hold regular meetings of the Chiefs of Defense staffs, and undertake closer military cooperation in the fields of logistics, transport, training, and strategic surveillance. Finally, they announced that they would transfer the WEU Secretariat and Council to Brussels from London.

The WEU's Role—Contending Formulations

In the aftermath of the Maastricht meetings, European leaders began to debate how to implement their "agreements" with an eye to the WEU spring 1992 ministerial meeting to be hosted by Germany. Since France was committed to a concept of European Union that included common defense, it naturally prompted the idea that the WEU should be closely tied to the European Council. Indeed, the prevailing French view in the spring of 1992 was that the Council, not the WEU, should be the primary forum for discussion and consensus-building on European political-military-security issues and that the WEU should limit its role to providing professional military advice and insights to the Council as needed. In a sense, France viewed the Maastricht formula for the role of the WEU as a kind of temporary stop on the way toward a common, European Union–based defense policy. For this reason, France proposed "dual-hatting" its permanent representative in Brussels to both the EC and the WEU. At the practical level, France's attention was focused more on developing the Franco-German Corps than on the possible roles to be played by the WEU outside the framework of the Corps.

By contrast, Britain and its Atlanticist allies stressed the other dimension of the Maastricht formula—strengthening the European pillar in the Alliance. British leaders viewed the WEU as complemen-

---

[38]WEU, Maastricht Declaration I, para. 2.

tary to NATO, available to act when NATO could or would not, but in all cases subordinate in matters of common defense. The British envisioned the WEU as a coordinating mechanism, able to respond in an ad hoc manner to contingencies. The Planning Cell would assume an operational role by drawing up contingency plans and conducting planning exercises as a means of preparing for possible actions, but the WEU would have no standing forces in peacetime, no permanent command structure, and no dedicated assets. To emphasize the WEU's links with NATO, the United Kingdom proposed co-locating the WEU planning cell with NATO planners at Mons, Belgium. Reflecting its general perspective on the WEU's role, Britain decided to dual-hat its NATO permanent representative to represent Britain in the WEU as well.

Germany fell somewhere in between the British and French views. German officials shared France's vision of a European Union that would embrace defense, a view consistent with Germany's continued emphasis on keeping its military forces integrated in multinational frameworks. Yet because of the internal political divisions surrounding the constitutional and prudential limits on the Bundeswehr's out-of-area activities, German officials were reticent to promote the WEU's role for activities beyond common defense. Moreover, Germany remained strongly committed to a continued U.S. military presence, which implied preserving a central control for NATO. Given the inherent tension in the German position, it is easy to see why Germany did not use its presidency of the WEU during the first half of 1992 to pursue aggressively the agenda set out at Maastricht.

Election setbacks for the governing coalition in Germany and the Socialists in France in early 1992, and the return of a Conservative government in the United Kingdom, tended to strengthen the hand of those who opposed a strong EC defense role, a result reinforced by Danish voters' opposition to the Maastricht Treaty and widespread disillusionment with an enhanced role for "Brussels."

The outline of a compromise began to emerge in May and June. The key elements grew out of a proposal by the new British Secretary of State for Defense, Malcolm Rifkind, in a speech to King's College on May 15, where he outlined ideas that he termed "the British contribution to a consensus which we hope will emerge" in the WEU.[39] Placing his remarks in the context of what European leaders had agreed to at Rome and Maastricht, Rifkind stressed the importance of developing a European security identity and defense role that reinforced the integrity and effectiveness of the Alliance, and that the WEU should be the focus for the emerging European defense capability. The WEU should remain independent of both the Atlantic Alliance and the European Union, but have close links to both.

Rifkind offered a rather expansive definition of the WEU mission. These included:

- Responses to threats in Europe, in instances where NATO chose not to be involved (an admittedly unlikely possibility in the case of major conflicts);

- International crisis management outside Europe where European interests are involved;

- Peacekeeping operations in Europe or elsewhere;

- Humanitarian and rescue missions.[40]

Rifkind's speech was one element of an aggressive campaign by the British to secure a desirable outcome at the WEU summit at Petersberg.[41]

The United States supported these efforts, both publicly and privately. The United States lobbied Germany heavily during May and June, including private letters from National Security Advisor Brent Scowcroft and others in the U.S. government to their counterparts in

---

[39]Malcolm Rifkind, "A Decade of Change in European Security," speech at King's College, London, May 14, 1992 (New York: British Information Services, Policy Statement 21/92), p. 8. Rifkind's speech was also intended, in all probability, to offer an explicit alternative to the model of the Eurocorps.

[40]Ibid. Rifkind did not specify, when referring to "Europe," whether he was referring to the NATO area only or meant to include out-of-area activities in Europe as well.

[41]An example of the British campaign is the article published by Rifkind in *Die Welt* on June 18, 1992, entitled "Give the WEU a Real Military Capacity Now." FBIS-WEU-92-120, June 22, 1992, p. 3.

Bonn.[42] Donald Atwood, Deputy Secretary of Defense, stated: "We look forward to continuing to work together to ensure that a strengthened European security and defense identity enhances the trans-Atlantic link, enables all of the European allies to participate fully in decisions affecting their security and does not detract from NATO's military effectiveness. In this regard, we support British Defense Minister Malcolm Rifkind's recent proposals on developing a military capability for the WEU, which would include the Franco-German Corps in a way that is fully compatible with our NATO objectives."[43]

The Petersberg Declaration

At its meeting at Petersberg in Bonn on June 19, the WEU issued a three-part declaration concerning the WEU and European security, the WEU's operational role, and the relationships between the WEU and other members of the European Union or the Atlantic Alliance. The WEU declared its willingness, once its operational capabilities are developed and in accordance with national procedures, to make forces available for conflict prevention or crisis management, including peacekeeping activities of the UN or the CSCE.[44] The declaration also reaffirmed the WEU's role as the defense component of the European Union and as the strengthened European pillar of the Atlantic Alliance. The WEU leaders called for practical steps to enhance coordination between the WEU, the EC, and NATO.[45] They also announced their intention to expedite the relocation of the Secretariat and the WEU Council from London to Brussels.

The WEU also finalized plans to develop its operational role. In formulations which echo many of Rifkind's recommendations, the WEU agreed to make forces available, in principle, for humanitarian and

---

[42]See "U.S., Bonn Clash over Pact with France," *Wall Street Journal,* May 27, 1992, p. A11.

[43]Donald J. Atwood, Address to a Conference on the Future of NATO, Washington, D.C., June 22, 1992.

[44]This formulation thus went beyond NATO's decision at its June 1992 Oslo meeting to make forces available for peacekeeping under CSCE auspices.

[45]Western European Union Council of Ministers, "Petersberg Declaration," Bonn, June 19, 1992, paras. I.2, I.9, and I.10 (hereinafter cited as Petersberg Declaration).

rescue missions, peacekeeping, or "tasks of combat forces in crisis management, including peacemaking."[46] The latter category represented a new willingness to consider involvement in contingencies that might require exposing military forces to greater levels of hostilities than traditional peacekeeping assignments, reflecting the growing awareness of the risk of conflict in the post–Cold War era along the lines of the fighting in former Yugoslavia.

According to the Petersberg Declaration, these peacekeeping and crisis management functions are "in addition to" contributing to the common defense, implying that the orientation of these activities is for contingencies outside the NATO area, in Europe or elsewhere. While noting that states would make such forces available "on a case-by-case basis and in accordance with our own procedures," the WEU also asked states for an inventory of units "from the whole spectrum of their conventional armed forces" to be available for such tasks.[47]

The Petersberg meeting also resolved the issue of non-WEU members' participation in WEU meetings and activities. Associate members—European states that belong to NATO but not the EC—may participate in WEU meetings and working groups, and join in implementing WEU decisions, unless a majority of WEU members vote to exclude them; they will have permanent liaison at the WEU Planning Cell, and will contribute to the WEU budget.[48] This decision broadly tracked the British view, which had argued for the broadest possible participation of non-WEU European NATO members, to assure the continued linkage between the WEU and NATO.

Implementing Petersberg

The WEU Planning Cell became operational in Brussels in October 1992, and began planning for contingencies consistent with the missions identified above. In asking members to make an inventory of "the whole spectrum of their conventional armed forces," the WEU left room for the Eurocorps to relate to the WEU through this pro-

---

[46]Ibid., para. II.4.

[47]Ibid., paras. I.2 and II.2.

[48]Petersberg Declaration, Part III, "On Relations Between WEU and Other European Member States of the European Union or the Atlantic Alliance," June 19, 1992.

cess. The Petersberg Declaration referred explicitly to the possibility that: "where multinational formations drawn from the forces of WEU nations already exist or are planned, these units could be made available for use under the authority of the WEU, with agreement of all participating nations."[49] The latter phrase protected both Germany's interest in avoiding out-of-area commitments until the Basic Law issue is resolved, and France's insistence on a national political decision prior to committing troops. This approach appears consistent with France's view, which has stated that, given the Corps' "European vocation," its priority is to act in the framework of the WEU under guidelines defined by the European Union.[50]

The Planning Cell will prepare contingency plans for employing forces and will keep an updated inventory of available forces. The Planning Cell will also prepare contingency plans and identify potential headquarters and necessary operating procedures for possible contingencies. The decision to locate the cell in Brussels will facilitate close liaison with NATO. The WEU leaders gave Chiefs of Defense staff responsibility to monitor the Planning Cell's work and to attend Council meetings whenever necessary. With the exception of the Planning Cell, the WEU created no permanent new organizational structures to implement the operational role. The WEU committed itself to conduct military exercises to further develop its operational capabilities.[51] The WEU also pledged to study further the possibility of creating a European Armaments Agency, consistent with the goal set at Maastricht of improving cooperation in the field of arms production. The first step in this direction was the decision to transfer the armaments cooperation activities of the Independent European Program Group (IEPG) to the WEU on December 4, 1992.[52]

---

[49]Ibid., para. II.7.

[50]"L'avènement du corps européen," p. 4.

[51]Petersberg Declaration, paras. II.8, II.9.

[52]See "WEU Bolsters Role in Defense," *Defense News*, December 7–13, 1992, p. 1. Under the WEU decision all IEPG members (including Norway, Iceland, and Turkey, not full members of the WEU) have full voting rights on arms cooperation issues.

The WEU's Evolving Operational Role

Until the mid-1980s, the WEU played no direct role in military operations. Following the revitalization of the WEU and the discussions leading to the adoption of the "Platform on European Security Issues" in 1987, the WEU began to play a more active in role in coordinating its members' military activities outside the NATO area, first in the Persian Gulf minesweeping operation (1987–1988) and later in enforcing the sanctions against Iraq following the 1990 invasion of Kuwait.[53]

During the early months following the outbreak of fighting in the former Yugoslavia in the summer of 1991, several WEU member states raised the issue of WEU intervention, either as peacekeepers or peacemakers, but there was no consensus in favor of WEU involvement. However, the WEU's formal decision at Petersberg to take on peacekeeping activities, coupled with the growing international activism in response to the fighting and the humanitarian crisis in Bosnia, led its leaders to send WEU naval forces to the Adriatic, initially to monitor the trade embargo against Serbia and Montenegro, and subsequently to enforce the embargo.[54] As the Security Council continued to tighten the sanctions in 1993, WEU-organized forces were also dispatched to monitor and enforce economic sanctions against traffic on the Danube.[55]

---

[53]For a description of the WEU's revitalization, see Robbin Laird, *The Europeanization of the Alliance*, Boulder, CO: Westview Press, 1991, Ch. 2, and Edward Mortimer, *European Security after the Cold War*, Adelphi Paper No. 271, International Institute for Strategic Studies, Summer 1992, pp. 55–63. For a detailed description of the 1987–88 minesweeping operation, see International Institute for Strategic Studies, *Strategic Survey 1987–88*, London, IISS, 1988, pp. 82–83.

[54]The WEU leaders took the initial decision to send naval forces on July 10, 1992, at a special meeting convened in the margins of a CSCE summit in Helsinki. At that meeting they also tasked experts to analyze the possibility of providing armed escorts for humanitarian relief. Eventually such a relief support effort was mounted, involving troops from France, Spain, the U.K., and Canada, but under UN rather than WEU auspices. The WEU decided to commit its forces to the blockade on November 20, 1992, following a November 16 Security Council Resolution and a similar decision by NATO on November 18.

[55]The WEU was expected to contribute 8–10 patrol boats and 250–300 individuals from France, Germany, Italy, Luxembourg, the Netherlands, and Spain. See "Owen calls for added pressure on Bosnian Serbs," *Financial Times*, April 6, 1993, p. 2.

The WEU naval force in the Adriatic included French, Italian, and Spanish warships, as well as German reconnaissance aircraft. NATO also mounted a naval operation, drawing on ships involved in STANAVFORMED, including U.S., Italian, German, British, and Turkish ships. Although both flotillas had similar missions, they were coordinated by dividing up the area of coverage (initially the NATO fleet was in the Southern Adriatic, while the WEU force patrolled the Strait of Otranto) with both fleets under Italian command.[56] After nearly a year of bifurcated operations, on June 8, 1993, NATO and the WEU agreed to establish a combined operation ("Sharp Guard") subject to the political control of both the NAC and the WEU Council of Ministers but with operational control under SACEUR (delegated to Commander Allied Naval Forces Southern Europe).[57]

THE EUROPEAN DEFENSE IDENTITY IN MID-1993

The proposed Eurocorps initially caused considerable consternation in several NATO capitals, notably London and Washington. Criticism of certain aspects of the Corps from these quarters was inevitable: it appeared to operate outside the framework of NATO; it could represent the creation of a duplicate, possibly even rival, structure for defense of the NATO area; it seemed at odds with agreements reached at Rome and at Maastricht; and the manner in which France and Germany developed the concept seemed the opposite of "transparency and complementarity."

Distrust of France's motives fueled American and British criticism. French advocates of a strong European defense capability argued that the United States will not maintain its military presence in Europe in the wake of the Soviet Union's collapse, and that Europe must act to fill the looming vacuum. While French officials repeatedly insisted that they did not seek such an outcome, France's critics pointed to its unwillingness to support actions to maintain NATO's relevance—and hence continued U.S. involvement in Europe—in the

---

[56]"8 Western Navies Cooperating in Watch on Yugoslav Coast," *Washington Post*, July 16, 1992.

[57]"Joint Session of the North Atlantic Council and the Council of the Western European Union held in Brussels on 8 June 1993," Press Release 93(41), June 8, 1993 (mimeo).

post–Cold War era. As a consequence, many in Washington and London interpreted France's actions as designed to undercut NATO. Even in Bonn, policymakers who are generally sympathetic to improved Franco-German military cooperation have difficulty explaining French resistance to initiatives such as the NACC.

Similarly, deep divisions between the Anglo-Italian and Franco-German conceptions of the WEU preoccupied the transatlantic debate through much of 1992. At a time when NATO remained uncertain, at the level of both theory and practice, as to just what role it would play in the post–Cold War world, there was a tendency to see any other structure, whether a West European Defense Identity or pan-European arrangements, as a mortal enemy.

Over the past two years, however, governments have begun to adopt a more pragmatic approach, concerned less with theoretical pronouncements than with dealing with problems at hand. This is attributable to a number of factors.

First, the WEU's Petersberg Declaration has proved a flexible accommodation that has allowed the WEU to begin to undertake administrative, planning, and even operational activities without forcing a confrontation over the long-run role of the WEU. With the Secretariat transferred to Brussels, the planning staff beginning its initial work, and the grouping of related European defense activities (IEPG, Eurogroup) under the WEU umbrella, the WEU is beginning to create institutional momentum that could form the basis for a more active role in the future. At the same time, co-location with NATO has allowed for a more informal, yet productive opportunity for building links between the two organizations. This can be seen in the January 27, 1993, decision of the two Secretaries General to establish a task force to improve communications between the two staffs.[58]

Second, France's evolving attitude toward European security institutions has facilitated pragmatic compromise. In particular, France—first under the Socialist government of Pierre Bérégovoy and later under RPR Prime Minister Eduard Balladur—has dropped its oppo-

---

[58]See "NATO Retains Authority in European Military Affairs, " *Defense News*, February 1–7, 1993, p. 3.

sition to NATO involvement beyond collective defense of allies' territory, and has begun to work with NATO structures in "out-of-area" missions. Not only has France participated under NATO operational control in enforcing the no-fly zone over Bosnia and as part of the Adriatic blockade of Serbia, but more broadly, France now actively participates in NATO's Military Committee on all issues related to peacekeeping. Moreover, French leaders have hinted at their willingness to consider even broader institutional participation, including perhaps some activities of the NACC and the DPC.

This is not to say that France is prepared to rejoin the integrated military command (French political leaders continue to rule that out), or that it has entirely lost interest in developing a European defense identity. But there is greater willingness to explore, on a case-by-case basis, effective operational solutions that take advantage of NATO's capabilities while respecting France's interest in preserving national and EC/WEU prerogatives.

Third, the tensions between the formation of the Eurocorps and both NATO and the WEU have eased as a result of understandings that will tend to limit the possibility of operational conflict. France and Germany have now more or less squarely set the Corps within the framework of the two institutions, to the considerable relief of their European and transatlantic partners. While issues remain concerning how and when the Eurocorps might be used, it is no longer a highly contentious (albeit theoretical) source of disagreement within the Alliance.

A fourth factor is the troubled course of European political union. One of the central issues in the initial Danish rejection of Maastricht was discomfort over the prospect of a common European defense. Events since the first Danish referendum have further clouded the outlook for moving toward a European defense identity based on the EC/European Union. The victory of the center-right coalition in France brought to power parties that have been less enthusiastic about ceding national authority to Brussels. Although most of the key national security posts have gone to the "Europeanist" wing of the UDF/RPR,[59] the new government seems less zealous in its desire

---

[59]François Léotard at Defense, Alain Juppé at the Foreign Ministry, and Alain Lamassoure at European Affairs.

to pursue a European-only approach. Thus, in his proposal for a new European conference on stability, Prime Minister Balladur explicitly included the United States and Canada, a distinct contrast with President Mitterrand's earlier proposal for a European confederation that did not include the United States.

The prospect of EC enlargement in the near future also raises doubts about the EC's future role in defense. Although the applicants have accepted in principle the Maastricht Treaty, with its commitment to the eventual development of a common defense policy, in practice their accession to the Community in the mid-1990s could make it more difficult to forge a consensus in favor of an active EC role. This in turn could have the effect of increasing support for maintaining the WEU as a separate organization—a "hard core" of states more inclined to act forcefully in the military dimension. Faced with the prospect of stalemate among the enlarged membership of the EC, France may come to see the virtue of an independent WEU that can act more decisively and quickly, thus bringing France closer to the British view.

Fifth, there is a growing awareness of the importance of maintaining direct U.S. involvement in Europe's post–Cold War security environment, on both a political and a military level. The experience of attempting to end the conflict in former Yugoslavia has convinced even the ardent European unionists that Europe will find it difficult to summon the political will and the military capability to handle ethnic and national conflict alone. While many continue to seek to strengthen Europe's independent capabilities (either as a hedge against unwanted U.S. withdrawal or as an incentive to continued U.S. involvement with more equitable burdensharing), few see a Europe-only solution, even for out-of-area, but in-Europe, contingencies.

Thus U.S. policy toward Europe, and toward the roles and responsibilities of any European defense identity, are likely to have a significant impact on the course of the EDI's evolution. How the United States has approached the issue in the past, and how it might proceed in the future, are the subject of the next chapter.

Chapter Four

THE UNITED STATES AND THE EUROPEAN DEFENSE IDENTITY

U.S. POLICY TO DATE

Throughout 1992, as Europe debated the role and organization of a European defense identity, the United States sought to shape the debate by articulating the U.S. view on European defense, especially the appropriate relationship between a European defense identity and the Atlantic Alliance. Although the United States has maintained that it is "up to the Europeans themselves" to decide how to organize their affairs, it has put forward, at times with great insistence, general criteria that (in the U.S. view) the EDI should meet.

Broadly speaking, the United States supported a strengthened European pillar of the Alliance and endorsed the WEU as the organizational locus for the EDI. It was less enthusiastic about a defense expression of European Union, having opposed in early 1991 a French-German proposal to subordinate the WEU to the European Council because the EC has no formal links to NATO. The United States was concerned by the risk that the EC could become a competitor organization to NATO. U.S. views closely paralleled the British concept for organizing European defense around the WEU, because the British approach met two principal U.S. objectives:

- Retain NATO's primacy, both as the forum for security consultations among members of the Alliance and as the exclusive means for organizing the defense of NATO members' territory.

- Strengthen Europe's ability to act out of area, either in partnership with the United States or alone if the United States chooses not to act.

In contrast, the United States expressed misgivings about the Euro-corps, on the grounds that it could challenge the primacy of NATO in the core area of territorial defense, loosen Germany's link to NATO, and establish an organization that at best duplicates, and at worst rivals, existing NATO functions.

U.S. objections to the Corps in early 1992 created serious frictions with France, and more subtle, but no less real, tensions with Germany.[1] The United States and the United Kingdom attempted to persuade Germany to move away from its commitment to the Corps, but with limited success. Germany sought repeatedly to assure the United States that the Corps posed no risk to U.S. interests or to the centrality of the Alliance. To many in the United States, the arguments that the Corps would not compete with NATO were unconvincing.[2] During the latter half of 1992, perhaps impelled by the rapidly worsening situation in former Yugoslavia and the growing political crisis in Russia, governments succeeded in overcoming or setting aside many of the initial disagreements concerning the Corps and its relationship to NATO. The result was the agreement in January 1993 between the Eurocorps and NATO.

This chapter explores options for U.S. policy toward the EDI in the future. It begins with a review of the strategic perspectives and objectives of Europe's dominant security actors—Britain, France, and Germany—then identifies long-term U.S. security interests in Europe and the implications of the EDI for those interests, and concludes with a proposed approach for U.S. policy toward the emerging European defense identity.

---

[1]See, for example, "Germans Caught in U.S.-French Rift," *Washington Post*, June 27, 1992, and "U.S.-French Relations Hit Rocks Over European Defense," *Christian Science Monitor*, June 5, 1992.

[2]An example is Jeane Kirkpatrick, "Eurocorps Shows Ambivalence About American Military Role," *Army*, July 1992, p. 12: "It all leads one to conclude that the main thing a Eurocorps would be that NATO is not is a multinational alliance of which the Americans could not be part."

European Strategic Perspectives That Shape EDI: The Context for U.S. Policy Toward the EDI

In formulating an approach toward the emerging EDI, U.S. policy must take into account varying national concerns and objectives that shape individual approaches to intra-European and transatlantic security relations.

France. The French approach to the European defense identity has evolved under the pressure of domestic political and international events since the debate leading up to Maastricht. Initially, France was motivated by two principal factors. First, many French analysts and senior government officials believed that the United States would inevitably, and in the not distant future, disengage from European security, despite U.S. assurances to the contrary. At La Rochelle, President Mitterrand voiced this concern: "We don't want to see American troops leave, but who knows what decisions will be made because of the economic difficulties facing the American leadership?"[3] The likelihood of U.S. withdrawal made it essential to develop alternative, European-only military capabilities to fill the void, as well as political structures to insure against the risk that Germany would feel obliged to develop its own national defense capability once it could no longer rely on the U.S. guarantee.

Second, French leaders believed that the collapse of communism and the Soviet empire provided a unique but short-lived opportunity to transform the European "common market" into a political union with responsibility for defense and security policy. Germany's zeal for demonstrating its European credentials was at its height in the immediate aftermath of German unification, and the Community remained at a relatively manageable size. Although de Gaulle's legacy led to some reluctance to accept political arrangements that would compromise French independence in matters of security, President Mitterrand and his advisers came to believe that without

---

[3]"France, Germany Unveil Corps as Step Toward European Defense," *Washington Post*, May 23, 1992.

the European Union, France would be unable to pursue its security interests, in Europe or outside.

These two factors led to a rather maximalist position on the European defense identity, at least on paper. But pragmatic considerations, beginning with the experience in the Gulf War and later in former Yugoslavia, tended to soften the European-only dogmatism. French leaders began to see that in some ways their global outlook brought them closer to the United States than their would-be partners in European defense identity. In particular, Germany's inability to resolve the question of participating in out-of-area operations, combined with deep Franco-German differences over Yugoslavia, led French leaders to diversify their approach to the future European security architecture, not only to accept a larger role for the United Nations and NATO, but also to accept closer links between France and NATO and the WEU and NATO.

These trends were apparent even before the change in government in March 1993. Under the Socialist government, France played an increasingly active role in NATO's Military Committee, participating fully in matters relating to peacekeeping.[4] In contrast to the contentious rhetoric of 1991 and early 1992, France and NATO authorities reached relatively easy agreement on the relationship between NATO and the Eurocorps, and, perhaps even more significantly, French aircraft operated under NATO operational control as part of Operation Deny Flight over Bosnia. (Later, under Prime Minister Balladur's government, French warships in the Adriatic would come under SACEUR's operational control as a result of the NATO/WEU agreement on enforcing the blockade against Serbia.)

The new government seems, if anything, even more open to pragmatic accommodation with NATO and transatlantic approaches to European security. While French leaders continue to stress the importance of developing a European defense identity, their concept focuses more on EDI as a complement, rather than alternative, to structures involving the United States. As noted earlier, Prime Minister Balladur's call for a European stability conference explicitly

---

[4]See "La France siége désormais avec voix délibérative au comité militaire de l'Otan," *Le Monde*, May 14, 1992, p. 5.

included the United States and Canada, in contrast to President Mitterrand's earlier concept for a European confederation.

The United Kingdom. The approach of the British government continues to stress the importance of the transatlantic dimension. Leaders of both major British parties remain unconvinced that a common defense within the context of a European Union is either desirable or even achievable. They therefore seek to retain the relevance of the Alliance to Europe and the relevance of Britain to the Alliance, a strategy they believe is likely to offer Britain greater influence than in an all-European structure.

At the same time, the experience of former Yugoslavia has led British leaders to conclude that, in the words of U.K. Foreign Secretary Douglas Hurd, "the United States may not automatically regard itself as involved in all sources of instability in Europe. There will be crises outside NATO territory in which we Europeans will wish to act, but that compulsion will not be so obvious across the Atlantic."[5]

Like France, Britain still retains a self-image as a global as well as a regional power. But unlike France, which has been multiplying its involvement in a broad range of "second generation" peacekeeping activities across the globe, in recent months British leaders have taken a more circumspect view of the future British role. Under the new British security concept, the principal emphasis of British defense planning will fall on two types of contingencies: homeland and overseas territory defense, and direct NATO collective defense commitments. Although British policy also contemplates a role in bringing about a "safer and more decent world," British involvement is likely to be much more limited: "we shall probably have to say 'no' more often than 'yes.'"[6]

These strategic considerations shape the British attitude toward the future European defense identity. First, NATO, not the European

---

[5]"The Role of NATO in the Post Cold War World," speech by Rt. Hon. Douglas Hurd, MP, to the Carlton Club Political Committee, June 30, 1993 (mimeo).

[6]The quotations are from Douglas Hurd's speech to the Royal Institute of International Affairs (Chatham House) on January 27, 1993. He added: "Obviously, we cannot be everywhere and we cannot do everything. Our diplomacy is now undermanned compared to that of our main colleague and competitors. Our armed forces are already stretched."

Union, will retain primary responsibility for collective defense of its members' territory. "NATO will not be supplanted by an independent European defense . . . NATO will continue to underpin the security of the European Union, even as and when the Union enlarges . . . In defence the transatlantic link and single military structure will remain vital." Second, European defense "coordination" should take place under the auspices of the WEU, rather than the Union itself. Third, the WEU should focus its activities on developing "a stronger European contribution . . . [w]hen NATO is involved," and on actions where Europe, but not the United States, decides to become engaged. Above all, the WEU should develop "gradually."[7]

Germany. Germany presents a third, more complicated perspective. Germany faces a complex set of challenges in coping with the consequences of unification. It has focused its energies on ensuring the withdrawal of Soviet forces from German territory and coping with an influx of refugees from the East and from the Balkans. The demands on German resources, in addition to the costs of unification, are high, including aid to Russia and financial support for international peacekeeping.

Germany supports the current evolution of NATO and does not urge radical restructuring. It also supports a broader political role for the Alliance, since, as the country bordering the former Warsaw Pact, Germany benefits directly from improved relationships and consultations such as those conducted in the NACC. Germany seeks—and is attaining—a larger role in NATO as an expression of its regained sovereignty; it also seeks to preserve NATO and the U.S. role, because that arrangement best serves German interests in dealing with the East.

Germany also has a strong political imperative to embed itself in Europe, to become a part of Europe-wide structures in order to allay fears of resurgent German power. It seeks close ties to France, a policy intended to demonstrate that Germany will never again threaten France. Finally, Germany is committed to European Union and to the EDI as a component of the Union, because, at least for

---

[7]These quotations are from Hurd's Carlton Club speech.

Chancellor Kohl, European Union is the permanent answer to the German question.[8]

Simultaneously pursuing all of these objectives, Germany is occasionally pulled in conflicting directions. The result is a German policy toward the EDI and other security institutions that contains the ambiguous or contradictory elements that surrounded the establishment of the Eurocorps. The conflicting impulses in German policy, pursuing at times European Union as the foremost objective, and at other times seeking a strong NATO, can be seen in the confusion over how German troops committed to the Corps would also retain their NATO responsibilities. The January agreement between the Eurocorps and NATO is emblematic of these conflicting impulses in German policy—close ties to France and unbreakable commitment to NATO—but the solution reached suggests that over time, developments in both France and Germany may reduce the apparent conflicts.

Underlying the ambiguity of Germany's position toward NATO and the EDI is the still unresolved question of Germany's participation in "out-of-area" military operations. Although Germany has supported both NATO and WEU moves to expand their missions beyond collective defense, and specifically identified noncollective defense missions for the Eurocorps, there is still no German political consensus in support of deploying German troops for these roles. This uncertainty in turn limits Germany's effectiveness in shaping the debate over the future of both NATO and the EDI.

Chancellor Kohl and members of his party have tried to resolve these ambiguities through advocacy and through a series of small *faits accomplis* that have gradually expanded the scope of the Bundeswehr's noncollective defense missions. On the level of rhetoric, the governing coalition pushed for a constitutional amendment that would explicitly permit the use of the Bundeswehr for peace enforcement missions not only under the UN but also under other multilateral arrangements, including NATO or the WEU (subject to a two-thirds

---

[8]See Wolfgang F. Schör, "German Security Policy," Adelphi Paper No. 277, London: IISS, Brassey's, 1993, pp. 25–27, 36–39.

majority in the federal parliament),[9] and Christian Democrat (CDU) defense policy leaders spoke out forcefully for a more active German role.

At the same time, Chancellor Kohl continued to test, case by case, the political and constitutional limits of the Bundeswehr's role. Beginning with the mine-sweeping operation in the Persian Gulf and humanitarian assistance to the Kurds after the war against Iraq, Germany continued to expand its out-of-area activities: a medical company as part of the UN military operation in Cambodia, a destroyer and three naval patrol aircraft as part of the NATO/WEU Adriatic deployment in connection with the sanctions against Serbia, participation of German officers in NATO AWACs in connection with Operation Deny Flight over Bosnia, and logistical support for the UN force in Somalia (UNISOM II). Although the constitutionality of some of these actions was challenged by the SPD (and, in the case of the AWACs participation, by the CDU's coalition partner, the Free Democrats (FDP)), the German Constitutional Court has thus far declined to intervene to block the deployments.

It is unlikely that the legal and political issue will be resolved definitively in the near future. The Constitutional Court has proved reluctant to issue sweeping judgments, preferring to try to encourage a political solution. While the SPD's attitude continues to evolve (there is a growing willingness to accept peace "enforcement" activities for the Bundeswehr, so long as they take place under Security Council mandate), there are still deep divisions among the rank and file, and little sentiment for going beyond UN-mandated actions. At best, the issue seems likely to remain open until after the next parliamentary elections in 1994. Until then, therefore, the German role in shaping the future role of EDI will remain ambiguous.

Over the long run, Germany is the key not only to the European defense identity, but to NATO and to the United States' military presence in Europe as well. Part of the U.S. criticism of the Eurocorps

---

[9]The proposal was offered on January 13, 1993, but it was opposed by many in the Social Democratic Party (SPD), some of whom would limit the Bundeswehr to traditional UN peacekeeping operations, while others would permit more expansive missions, but only under UN mandate. See "Preparation for Bundeswehr Combat Missions," *Frankfurter Allgemeine Zeitung,* January 14, 1993, pp. 1–2, FBIS-WEU-93-010, January 15, 1993, pp. 15–17.

stemmed from the sense that Germany was turning away from its close relationship with the United States, a belief that Germany had momentarily lost its focus on the importance of NATO as the anchor for any new security architecture and was also showing ingratitude for the United States' unwavering support for German unification.[10]

Other European States. The remaining members of the EC remain divided over the emphasis they place on the development of a European defense identity. Denmark lies at one extreme: concerns over a potential obligation to take part in EDI contributed to the initial Danish rejection of Maastricht, and Denmark continues to refuse membership in the WEU.[11]   Denmark's Atlanticist leanings are shared to a greater or lesser extent by Portugal and the Netherlands. Belgium, now the third nation to participate in the Eurocorps, shows much greater enthusiasm about a strong EDI, but its rapidly shrinking military capability means that its support is more political than operational. Spain, too, seems likely to join the Eurocorps, and is already participating with France in more closely linked European naval operations in the Mediterranean.[12] Italy stands in the middle, enthusiastic for a deeper European Union, and closely linked to France and Spain on Mediterranean security issues, yet still joined with the United Kingdom in its strategy for developing the WEU (in part out of concern that Italian interests would be secondary in a Franco-German led EDI).

The prospect that the EC will soon enlarge its membership is likely to have a significant impact on the course of EDI's evolution. Although some political leaders among the potential new applicants (especially in Austria) have raised the issue of joining the WEU as well as the Community, the next round of enlargement (likely to embrace Austria, Finland, Norway, and Sweden) will probably mean growing discrepancy between the membership of the EC and WEU. This will complicate the prospects for merging the WEU into the EC,

---

[10]See William Pfaff, "It Came to a Decision, and Germany Chose Paris," *Baltimore Sun,* June 4, 1992, p. 11.

[11]Ireland, traditionally neutral, has also declined membership in the WEU, but has not sought to block other EC nations from giving the Community a defense dimension.

[12]Greece, the newest member of the WEU, appears to support a relatively robust concept of the EDI, but this seems as much as a means of gaining support for its ongoing struggles with Turkey as part of articulating a comprehensive role for the EDI.

especially since enlargement is likely to precede the Maastricht-established date (1996) for addressing this issue. The probable reluctance of at least some of the new EC members to promote a robust EDI may lead even France to accept a "variable geometry" for the EDI, one that does not include all members of the European Union.[13]

Given these differing perspectives and motivations concerning the defense dimension of European Union, it will not be surprising if arguments and debates surrounding the European defense identity persist as an important issue in the transatlantic dialogue. The fact that the Europeans have divergent views provides the opportunity for the United States to play a constructive role in shaping the outcome of the debate in a way that advances U.S. as well as European objectives. In formulating a policy toward the EDI, the United States should pursue a two-pronged strategy, fostering the evolution and adaptation of NATO, and shaping the emerging European defense identity in ways compatible with U.S. interests. Taking into account the unique perspectives and political constraints of individual Allies will be an important requirement for the success of such a strategy.

U.S. Objectives in Europe

In the post–Cold War era, the United States continues to have enduring security objectives in Europe:

- Prevent the emergence of a direct threat to the United States.

- Preserve the security and stability of the Euro-Atlantic area.

- Maintain and strengthen the U.S.-European partnership in responding to security problems outside Europe.

---

[13]At the June 1993 Copenhagen summit, the EC took further steps toward the eventual goal of admitting at least some East European countries (particularly Poland, Hungary, and the Czech and Slovak republics). Their prospective membership should pose fewer problems for developing the EDI. These countries have already developed links to the WEU (in connection with the decision of the June 1992 WEU Council meeting at Petersberg), and while they also have strong interests in maintaining an effective transatlantic tie through their eventual membership in NATO, they see the two processes as complementary.

- Retain U.S. influence to shape European national and multi-lateral policies in a way that will promote U.S. global political and economic interests.

- Reduce the U.S. burden associated with European defense.

These longstanding objectives remain relevant despite a security environment dramatically different from that of the preceding forty years. But it will be necessary to formulate new policies and adapt security institutions in order to achieve these objectives under changed circumstances. The possibility of a direct threat has receded, but the United States needs to hedge against the re-emergence of a hostile superpower military rival and to limit the proliferation of weapons of mass destruction that could threaten the United States (or its allies). The United States' interest in European political and economic stability is somewhat more attenuated in an era where small conflicts are less likely to ignite world war. Instability is still corrosive, however, and could lead to an environment in which large-scale conflict becomes more likely, democratic governments become less stable (due to external political pressures, the challenges of immigration and refugees, and economic strains), and the pressure to renationalize defense ignites dangerous new arms races. Although the end of the Cold War has broken some of the linkages that tied conflicts out of Europe to the central East-West confrontation, the United States and Europe still have common interests in non-European crises, as the Gulf War amply demonstrates. Preserving U.S. influence is a more demanding challenge today, since Europe is less dependent on U.S. security guarantees (conventional and nuclear), and more on a par with the United States economically, often with competing interests, as the disputes over the Uruguay Round of GATT negotiations amply demonstrate. Thus American influence on European policy decisions will depend more on cooperative structures, political ties, and shared perceptions of common interests than on European dependence on the United States.

The United States cannot achieve its objectives acting in isolation from its allies, nor is it likely that the United States, acting alone, can determine the course of all key developments affecting U.S. interests. Further, it is no longer appropriate to maintain the Cold War division of roles and responsibilities between Europe and the United States. In an era when the direct threats to U.S. interests in Europe are more remote, when the United States must continue to shoulder global responsibilities, and when Europe is more capable of handling a greater economic and military share of the burden, a reallocation of responsibilities is not only appropriate but will probably be insisted on by the American public. Many Europeans will also demand a more equal partnership on questions of security.

The United States cannot leave the objective of preserving European security up to the Europeans alone, however, for at least three reasons. First, there is the risk that no effective European defense identity will arise (given the differing perspectives of key European actors), raising the prospect that conflicts in Europe will go unchecked, instability will spread, and nations will renationalize defense. Ironically, a hands-off policy by the United States could make this result more rather than less likely, since by playing a constructive and engaged role the United States can help mediate conflicts among the Europeans themselves and thus foster European security coordination. Second, if a European defense identity did emerge without U.S. involvement, it would probably have significant military deficiencies, limiting its effectiveness or requiring it to duplicate capabilities that the United States and NATO could contribute—undesirable if not infeasible at a time when defense resources are already stretched thin. Finally, an EDI developed without U.S. involvement is more likely to be indifferent to or, at worst, opposed to U.S. goals and policies. For all of these reasons, the United States has a substantial national security interest in seeing the development of a credible defense identity in Europe, able to serve as an effective partner or to act on its own where the United States chooses not to participate.

To achieve its objectives over the longer term, the United States will therefore need to develop new arrangements with its European allies. A two-pronged strategy—fostering the evolution of NATO while seeking to shape the EDI in ways compatible with U.S. interests—provides the basic approach. Such an approach should be sustainable over the longer term, responsive to the differing perspectives of the European actors, and flexible enough to meet the unforeseen political developments on that continent.

Elements of U.S. Policy

There are five key elements to a U.S. policy based on encouraging NATO's adaptation and on shaping the EDI:

(1) Continue to support the EDI.

(2) Continue to work to shape the Eurocorps' development in ways that are compatible with NATO and with U.S. security interests.

(3) Adapt NATO to embrace an effective EDI and build links between the EDI and NATO.

(4) Begin to identify the respective roles of NATO and the EDI, but avoid establishing formal or binding criteria.

(5) Try to preserve the congruence in membership between NATO and the EDI, but accept that the EDI can become the defense arm of the EC.

1. Continue support for EDI. The basic motivations that led to U.S. support for a European pillar in defense since the 1960s remain relevant today, as the United States seeks to redistribute the burden of Alliance defense and to reduce its troop presence in Europe. A strengthened European pillar can provide a basis for reducing the American burden for NATO territorial defense and free up the shrinking pool of U.S. troops for use in other contingencies and roles. Of perhaps greater significance in the post–Cold War era, a strengthened European pillar can provide the United States with a capable partner for operations outside the traditional NATO area, in Europe and beyond. A well-developed EDI with an operational role could also provide an alternative for actions in contingencies when the United States chooses not to act, especially in regional conflicts in Europe itself, contingencies that may prove increasingly likely in the coming years.

2. Continue to work to shape the Eurocorps. There are several compelling reasons to accept the establishment of the Eurocorps, rather than adamantly opposing it as inimical to U.S. interests. First, a policy of outright opposition, which was unsuccessful in preventing the initial establishment of the Corps, would also be unlikely to succeed in affecting its future development, at least at an acceptable political price. The Corps is a high political priority for Chancellor Kohl and

President Mitterrand, despite its somewhat contradictory conceptual underpinnings, and the two leaders have committed their prestige to making a go of it. As discussed in Chapter Three, the Corps serves fundamental political objectives in both countries.

Second, continued U.S. opposition would only antagonize an important ally, Germany, and indirectly confirm the French view that the United States does not want Europe to decide its defense organization for itself. Third, the risk posed by the Corps—to NATO and to a broader EDI based on the WEU and linked to NATO—is small. The Corps will not become operational for years; much can happen in the meantime, including the emergence of new leadership in both France and Germany.[14] The resources devoted to it are limited, and the forces most likely to be assigned are heavy forces with little utility outside territorial defense anyway. Finally, encouraging Franco-German military cooperation is in the United States' interest, because it will promote the essential stability of Europe. The Corps could contribute toward keeping Germany integrated with and tied to its neighbors, expanding France's linkage to NATO, and harnessing the two key West European military forces for future collective action under a variety of institutional auspices, including the UN and CSCE.

To accept the Corps is not be indifferent to its composition or operation. Even symbolic political acts without real military capability could, over time, weaken rather than enhance Western security. The agreement between the Eurocorps and SACEUR can be seen as a concrete step to insure that the Corps does not become either a competitor to NATO or militarily irrelevant. To the extent that the practice of incorporating the Corps and the French forces assigned to it into NATO contingency planning and military exercises becomes a routine occurrence, much of the traditional French distance from NATO's military command will have been overcome. If this occurs— and it is in the United States' interest to seek it—the German argu-

---

[14]French positions on European defense are not tied to Mitterrand, of course, but the Kohl-Mitterrand personal relationship was an important factor in setting up the Corps. In Germany, the defense spokesman of the opposition SPD party called the Corps a "militarily useless effort," and another SPD Bundestag member referred to the Corps as "the first army that has spread fear and terror even before it was deployed." "Agreement on Bundeswehr Participation in UN Missions," *Frankfurter Allgemeine*, June 11, 1992, in FBIS-WEU-92-114, p. 12.

ment that the Eurocorps binds France closer to NATO will be validated and a large number of rather tiresome "theological" disputes about the future structure of European security may no longer clog the strategic debate.

As the Eurocorps develops, it will be important to clarify its relationship to the WEU and to other participating European forces. It seems unlikely that large numbers of other forces will sign on to the Corps at present, but the ability of the WEU Planning Cell, the Eurocorps planning staff, and NATO's planners at SHAPE to develop meaningful consultative arrangements should be a priority for all three organizations.

3. Adapt NATO to embrace an effective EDI and build links between the EDI and NATO. NATO has set in motion a reform and restructuring process that will not be complete before 1995. These changes are not trivial, but they are unlikely to be sufficient to ensure the Alliance's continued relevance. The new Strategic Concept and its associated military strategy were adopted prior to the demise of the Soviet Union and the intensification of ethnic conflict in the Balkans and beyond. Barring a resurgent threat comparable to that posed by the Soviet Union, NATO's planned command and force structure may prove difficult to justify by 1995. This will be especially true for the United States. The current posture was predicated on the presence of 150,000 U.S. troops and a Corps structure capable of performing the Main Defense mission in NATO, but that assumption is already out of date.[15] If the United States and its NATO Allies were to cling to a vision of NATO as a slightly reduced version of the Alliance that won the Cold War, there is a danger that NATO will appear increasingly irrelevant to European security requirements of the late 1990s.

For these reasons, continuing the Alliance's adaptation process is in the United States' interest. This adaptation needs to take place on both the political and the operational level. For the United States,

---

[15]The U.S. Congress has indicated several times, most recently in a vote in the House of Representatives on the Fiscal Year 1993 Defense Authorization bill, its support for troop levels no greater than 100,000. The Clinton Administration has announced that U.S. forces in Europe will be reduced to 75,000 to 100,000, rather than the 150,000 pledged by the previous administration.

the Alliance's political function is critical; it is the primary forum for transatlantic consultation on questions of security, and this consultative role should be maintained. There is a certain tension between this objective and a stronger EDI. As the EDI, and more generally, the EC's common foreign and security policy develop, Europeans will consult more frequently among themselves prior to engaging in the NATO forum, and NATO will be seen as "the place you go to talk to the Americans." This should be acceptable to the United States as long as the Alliance is a forum for genuine discussion and dialogue. The objective of the United States must be consultation on and participation in all decisions that could affect U.S. interests—even if in the end the European Allies choose to undertake actions without U.S. participation and even without U.S. concurrence. The United States will not sustain a security commitment to Europe if Europeans regularly act without consulting the United States first.

In pursuing this objective, the United States must recognize that reciprocity will be required. U.S. allies will be less willing to follow U.S. initiatives if they are not consulted beforehand. With the demise of a rival superpower, the unique capabilities of the United States, which led Europeans to defer to it in the past, are less significant. In these circumstances, the United States must accept a more balanced role in the Alliance.

The stress on continued and improved consultation as a component of NATO's adaptation is more than rhetoric, because it will be very difficult to establish in advance agreed procedures governing relations between the EDI, whatever its institutional form, and the Alliance. As an example, some in NATO had hoped to establish the principle that NATO should have the "right of first refusal," allowing NATO to decide whether to take responsibility for a military operation. Only if NATO declined would the lead fall to the WEU. Such an arrangement cannot be codified. In practice, given NATO's decisionmaking by consensus procedures and France's broad opposition (at least in the past) to NATO's missions beyond the traditional Article V defense of NATO territory, France (or any other European country) will always be able to determine under which institutional auspices the decisions are taken. Effective consultative procedures are the only alternative to a breakdown in cooperation.

The consultative role must also evolve with relation to non-NATO members. The NACC has been successful to date in providing a forum for discussing security matters with former members of the Warsaw Treaty Organization. As the new architecture of European security is more fully elaborated, the role of NACC is likely to change. Some "liaison partners" may become members of the EC or the WEU, and some might even seek membership in NATO. Non-NACC neutrals may seek more formal consultative links (Finland's association with NACC could be a forerunner). The CSCE could well provide the umbrella for most discussions with former Soviet republics. In some areas, however, the NACC may continue to perform a unique role: for example, consultations concerning cooperative action for peacekeeping operations, defense policy, and civil-military relations in the former Communist countries.

NATO must also adapt on the organizational level. The objective here is three-fold:

- Ensure that NATO can operate in a militarily effective way in the face of new operational challenges.

- Make sure that all Allies can fight together—in and out of area—in an era with fewer U.S. stationed troops and curtailed budgets.

- Give Europeans the operational capability to act alone, at least for small-to-medium conflicts and peacekeeping or humanitarian operations.

Key steps include:

- Greater flexibility to mix and match forces to suit varying contingencies.

- U.S. force contributions that maximize unique U.S. advantages (lift, surveillance, high-technology weapon systems).

- A close link between U.S. forces in Europe and the ARRC, the most-likely-to-be-used force.

- A distinctive European identity within NATO forces that would allow independent European action while maintaining ties to the North American partners.

This final point deserves some elaboration.

The easiest way to permit independent European action without wasteful duplication is through the creative use of dual-hatting that creates a shadow European organization consistent with NATO force structures and command arrangements. The nucleus of this approach could be formed around NATO's new command structure—with the European Deputy SACEUR (now a British general) and Chief of Staff (German) ready to wear the dual hat of WEU Commander and Chief of Staff, respectively. European force contributions to NATO should be "detachable" for Europe-only operations (such as the U.K.-Netherlands amphibious force). For French forces outside the integrated military command, the current agreements that govern French-NATO cooperation should be modified to fit the emerging Eurostructure, just as the agreement between NATO and the Eurocorps reflects these emerging realities.[16] NATO should facilitate exercising the European element of the Alliance, using the WEU planning staff as well as fighting forces. The interoperability could be further enhanced by dual-hatting European planners to SHAPE and the WEU, or at least cross-placement of WEU planners at SHAPE and vice versa.

4. Begin to differentiate the roles of the EDI and NATO. In the end, structural adaptation will matter only insofar as NATO is willing to engage in the security problems of the day. But finding a new operational role for NATO raises difficult questions over what is the proper role for NATO, and what for the EDI. This problem has already ripened in the area of peacekeeping.

Both the WEU and NATO have now offered to make resources available for participation in peacekeeping operations under the auspices of the UN and CSCE. Indeed, the WEU spoke of a more robust concept of "peacemaking" and crisis management at Petersberg, although it failed to define these activities in detail.

Peacekeeping and the more amorphous "peacemaking" illustrate the divergent perspectives of the Allies and the tensions surrounding the efforts both to create the EDI and to ensure NATO's continued relevance through adaptation to new roles. Decisions to engage in

---

[16]A similar approach is hinted at by Pierre LeLouche in *Le Figaro*, July 23, 1992, p. 5.

peacekeeping activities will require decisions about when NATO will act out of area as an Alliance, something France has traditionally opposed. With a veto in the UN Security Council, and the ability to block consensus in both the CSCE and the NAC, France can effectively limit NATO's role if it so chooses. Germany has not yet resolved its own political and legal barriers to engage in peacekeeping and other out-of-area actions, although the governing coalition is pushing hard to make such participation possible. The British, with their own experiences in Cyprus and Northern Ireland, are extremely reluctant to intervene in ethnic or sectarian violence, noting that peacekeeping runs the risk of becoming peace enforcement. The United States has not yet seriously addressed the issue of how and when it will use its own forces, especially its ground forces, in peacekeeping operations, including any NATO might undertake.

So who peacekeeps when, and who decides? The problem is not academic; the presence of both NATO and WEU operations in the Adriatic monitoring the embargo against Serbia (now resolved through the creation of a single force under the operational control of SACEUR) illustrates the potential for conflict, duplication, and even tragedy from confused lines of responsibility and authority. Although NATO "doctrine" on peacekeeping is carefully hedged ("case by case . . . in accordance with our own procedures"), as a practical matter, NATO's role has grown dramatically over the past year in the context of continuing conflict in the former Yugoslavia. This has ranged from "shadow" contributions (elements of NATO's now disbanded NORTHAG headquarters were dispatched to help form the UN's Bosnia headquarters, although there is no formal NATO operational involvement) to direct use of the NATO chain of command for operational control as well as NATO military assets (enforcement of the no-fly zone over Bosnia, the combined Adriatic command, air support for the UN forces in Bosnia). Moreover, NATO, through the NACC, has moved to expand its involvement in peacekeeping/peace enforcement operations with non-NATO nations, through the NACC Ad Hoc Group on Cooperation in Peacekeeping.[17] The WEU, though a frequent forum for political-military consultations, has played a more limited operational role:

---

[17]See, e.g., "Report to Ministers by the NACC Ad Hoc Group on Cooperation in Peacekeeping," Press Release M-NACC-1(93)40, June 11, 1993.

part of the Adriatic fleet (now subsumed under SACEUR's operational control) and the Danube sanctions enforcement mission.

Although Yugoslavia suggests that NATO, for political and operational reasons, is likely to play the principal role in "out-of-area" peacekeeping operations, this arrangement may not prove sustainable over the medium term. The U.S. reluctance first to become involved at all in the Yugoslavia conflict, and later to commit ground forces, foreshadows what is almost certain to be a less directly engaged U.S. military role in Europe. Thus if Europeans wish to use military force or forces in preventing or managing Yugoslav-type or smaller crises in the future, they will more likely have to rely on their own capabilities and institutions. Still, in most cases, Europeans will want to have the United States "waiting in the wings" as a hedge against crisis escalation. Thus, under the most likely circumstances, the WEU might evolve into the operational tool of first resort, especially for small crises and conflict prevention.

But it would be undesirable to create a rigid formula, "first the WEU, then NATO," for a number of reasons. First, even for small conflicts, NATO, by virtue of U.S. participation, will possess valuable capabilities (such as intelligence collection and dissemination) that the WEU is unlikely to possess even in the longer term. Second, the participation of the United States even at early stages of the conflict sends a strong political signal that may help prevent the conflict from escalating. Third, the United States has a strong interest participating "in the takeoff" if Europeans hope to count on the U.S. "for the landing" if the conflict worsens.

This suggests two conclusions. First, it is essential that EDI/WEU states consult with the United States even on limited peacekeeping missions before deciding to become involved, even if the United States has no veto or formal role in the decisionmaking process. At the same time, the United States must accept a rather expansive concept of when it will become involved in European crises, even where the conflict does not directly and obviously affect U.S. interests. If the United States does not demonstrate reasonable availability to participate with its European allies in subregional crises, it is likely that Europeans will rely increasingly on European-only structures to manage these conflicts, to the detriment of NATO operational capabilities and political sustainability.

Thus the answer to the respective roles and responsibilities of NATO and the EDI will depend to an important extent on how the United States defines its security interests in Europe in the future. Similarly, the evolving perspectives of key European states will affect the outcome.

But an agreed conceptual approach is preferable, and the realities are that France, as much as other Europeans, will want U.S. involvement in most cases, particularly if the U.S.-European relationship becomes more equal. Indeed, the problem is at least as likely to be the opposite—U.S. unwillingness to participate. Thus to keep NATO relevant in this area, the United States must make clear its political stake in European stability (as it was reluctant to do in Yugoslavia) and commit to using U.S. forces—including, where appropriate, U.S. ground forces—in European peacekeeping operations.

Here the operational links become especially important, so that the United States and its European allies can peacekeep and act together or separately. There is therefore a need to develop operational links between the WEU and NATO for peacekeeping and peacemaking. Developing common operational concepts and military doctrine as well as training forces for these missions is an essential first step.

5. Try to preserve the congruence in membership between NATO and the EDI, but accept that the EDI could become the defense arm of the EC. Some in the United States and Europe (especially in the United Kingdom) have insisted that the only way to maintain EDI's compatibility with transatlantic structures is to keep it separate from the EC (or "European Union"). This fear seems misplaced. In the first place, linking security and defense to the EC can help deepen European integration, a longstanding U.S. objective that remains relevant today. If a "European Army" under the auspices of a European Defense Community made sense in 1954, it surely does now, when avoiding nationalist conflicts and the renationalization of defense is one of the most important European security objectives and the United States is withdrawing the bulk of its forces from Europe.

There are some costs to this approach. Deeper political/military integration under the EC will mean that the United States has diminished opportunities for carrying out bilateral policies and operations, as it did with Britain in the bombing of Libya in 1986. But the United States also pays a price for the fragmented European response that comes from a weak common European foreign and security policy.

Of course, the Europeans themselves might ultimately decide to keep EDI separate from the Union; even strong integrationists such as France are concerned that an enlarged EC will be ineffective in security policy, and may wish to retain a "hard core" [*noyau dur*] of West European nations (perhaps centered around the WEU) for defense cooperation.

Although the United States could benefit if the Europeans link defense to the European Union, U.S. interests would be harmed if, as a result of this link, core European nations refused to broaden their security cooperation to the emerging democracies in Eastern Europe. For this reason, the United States should support extending EC political, economic, and military ties to the East, with the ultimate goal of EC membership for those former Communist countries that make the successful transition to democratic government and market economies. At the same time, if the EC expands, and that expansion means that new EC members become part of the EDI, the United States should support parallel expansion of NATO, so that the security guarantees of the Brussels Treaty and participation in EDI are coextensive with the NATO guarantees. This will help avoid the situation where some but not all NATO allies are bound to defend other European states by virtue of their membership in the EC. Of course, this entails expanding U.S. security commitments on the European continent, but the alternative means a greater disjunction between the United States and its European allies.

At the same time, the United States should stress the need for WEU Europeans to involve the non-WEU European NATO members (Norway, Iceland, Denmark, and Turkey), to assure that these NATO allies are not marginalized by the elaboration of the EDI. The compromise agreed at Petersberg in June 1992, for broad-ranging participation of these countries as WEU associate members, is a constructive step in this direction.

Chapter Five

CONCLUSION

The issue of a European defense identity is a perennial plot line in the longrunning transatlantic security story.[1] Like the childhood tale of the three bears, the issue is often seen as how to get the balance "just right": neither too cold (a weak Europe dependent on and free riding under a U.S.-provided security umbrella) nor too hot (Euro-centric structures that disrupt the transatlantic link). In fact, done right, European cooperation and an effective European defense identity can be a net gain to all partners, as John Foster Dulles perceived in supporting the European Defense Community in 1954. For the United States in 1993, the greater risk is not a powerful, exclusive EDI, but rather a Europe that has lost the will and means to cope effectively with regional and global crises. In the past, the United States has depended on strong individual European partners, notably Britain and France, to carry the global security role, while Germany provided a key share of the European territorial defense. But political and economic forces make it less and less likely that these "medium" powers, acting alone, can make a substantial contribution. Only through a more integrated European effort—one that still retains important transatlantic ties (although not necessarily a "European Army" as some in the early 1950s imagined)—can the U.S. hope both to share burdens and to meet the far-flung and diverse security challenges in the years ahead.

---

[1] For some earlier chapters of the saga, see Alistair Buchan, *NATO in the 1960s*, London: IISS, 1962; and Jonathan Alford and Kenneth Hunt (eds.), *Europe in the Western Alliance: Towards a European Defence Identity?* New York: St. Martin's Press, 1988. For a largely European perspective on the contemporary debate, see Peter Schmidt (ed.), *In the Midst of Change: On the Development of West European Security and Defence Cooperation*, Baden Baden: Nomos Verlaggesellschaft, 1992.